ASSESSING
ASSESSMENT

7-DAY LOAN

Stamp indicates date for return

This item may be renewed if not required by another customer

To renew, use the library catalogue or tel: 0113 343 5663

Fines will be charged for late returns

ASSESSING ASSESSMENT

Series Editor:
Harry Torrance, University of Sussex

The aim of this series is to take a longer term view of current developments in assessment and to interrogate them in terms of research evidence deriving from both theoretical and empirical work. The intention is to provide a basis for testing the rhetoric of current policy and for the development of well-founded practice.

ASSESSING
ASSESSMENT

EVALUATING AUTHENTIC ASSESSMENT

PROBLEMS AND POSSIBILITIES IN NEW APPROACHES TO ASSESSMENT

Edited by Harry Torrance

Open University Press
Buckingham · Philadelphia

Open University Press
Celtic Court
22 Ballmoor
Buckingham
MK18 1XW

and

1900 Frost Road, Suite 101
Bristol, PA 19007, USA

First Published 1995
Reprinted 1996

A catalogue record of this book is available from the British Library

ISBN 0 335 19342 0 (pb) 0 335 19343 9 (hb)

Library of Congress Cataloging-in-Publication Data
Evaluating authentic assessment : problems and possibilities in new
    approaches to assessment / edited by Harry Torrance.
        p.   cm. – (Assessing assessment)
    Includes bibliographical references and index.
    ISBN 0–335–19343–9   ISBN 0–335–19342–0 (pbk.)
    1. Educational tests and measurements – Great Britain –
Evaluation.   2. Educational evaluation – Great Britain.
I. Torrance, Harry.   II. Series.
LB3056.G7E85   1994
371.2'6'0941 – dc20   94–27673
                                                                    CIP

Typeset by Colset Private Ltd, Singapore
Printed and bound in Great Britain by
Biddles Ltd, Guildford and King's Lynn

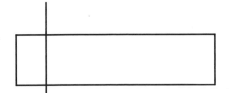

CONTENTS

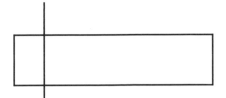

LIST OF
CONTRIBUTORS

Patricia Broadfoot is Professor of Education and Director of the Centre for Assessment Studies in the School of Education, University of Bristol. She was Co-Director of the Records of Achievement National Evaluation and Co-Director of the ESRC-funded study 'Implementing the National Curriculum in Primary Schools'.

Margaret Brown is Professor of Mathematics Education in the Centre for Educational Studies, King's College, University of London. She was Co-Director of the ESRC-funded evaluation 'National Assessment in Primary Schools'.

Caroline Gipps is a Professor of Education at the University of London Institute of Education. She was Co-Director of the ESRC-funded evaluation 'National Assessment in Primary Schools'.

Shelley McAlister was a Research Officer on the 'National Assessment in Primary Schools' evaluation and is a tutor in Social Policy at the Open University.

Bet McCallum was a Research Officer on the 'National Assessment in Primary Schools' evaluation and is tutor to the Advanced

Diploma in Curriculum Studies and the Primary School at the University of London Institute of Education.

Hilary Radnor is a Senior Lecturer in Education in the School of Education, University of Exeter. She was Director of the 'Moderation and Assessment Project – South West'.

Ken Shaw is a Senior Lecturer in Education in the School of Education, University of Exeter and was Evaluator to the 'Moderation and Assessment Project – South West'.

Harry Torrance is a Senior Lecturer in Education and Director of Research in the Institute of Continuing and Professional Education, University of Sussex. He is Director of the ESRC-funded project 'Teacher Assessment at Key Stage 1'.

Alison Wolf is a Reader in Education at the University of London Institute of Education and Co-Director of the International Centre for Research on Assessment based at the Institute.

SERIES EDITOR'S INTRODUCTION

Changing theories and methods of assessment have been the focus of significant attention for some years now, not only in the United Kingdom, but also in many other western industrial countries and many developing countries. Curriculum developers have realized that real change will not take place in schools if traditional paper-and-pencil tests, be they essay or multiple choice, remain unchanged to exert a constraining influence on how teachers and pupils approach new curricula. Similarly, examiners have been concerned to develop more valid and 'authentic' ways of assessing the changes which have been introduced into school syllabuses over recent years – more practical work, oral work, problem solving and so forth. In turn, psychologists and sociologists have become concerned with the impact of assessment on learning and motivation, and how that impact can be developed more positively. This has led to a myriad of developments in the field of assessment, often involving an increasing role for the teacher in school-based assessment, as more relevant and challenging tasks are devised by examination agencies for administration by teachers in schools, and as the role and status of more routine teacher assessment of coursework, practical work, groupwork and so forth have become enhanced.

However, educationists have not been the only ones to focus much more closely on the interrelation of curriculum, pedagogy and assessment. Governments around the world have also begun to take a close interest in the ways in which assessment can influence and even control teaching, and in the changes in curriculum and teaching which could be brought about by changes in assessment. This interest has not been wholly coherent. Government intervention in the UK has sometimes initiated, sometimes reinforced the move towards a more practical and vocationally orientated curriculum and thus the move towards more practical, school-based assessment. But government has also been concerned with issues of accountability and with what it sees as the maintenance of traditional academic standards through the use of externally set tests.

It is precisely because of this complexity and confusion that the present series of books on assessment has been developed. Many claims are being made with respect to the efficacy of new approaches to assessment which require careful review and investigation. Likewise, many changes are being required by government intervention which may lead to hurried and poorly understood developments being implemented in schools. The aim of this series is to take a longer-term view of the changes which are occurring, to move beyond the immediate problems of implementation and to interrogate the claims and the changes in terms of broader research evidence which derives from both theoretical and empirical work. In reviewing the field in this way, the intention of the series is thus to highlight relevant research evidence, identify key factors and principles which should underpin the developments taking place, and provide teachers and administrators with a basis for informed decision-making which takes the educational issues seriously and goes beyond simply accommodating the latest policy imperative.

This latest volume in the series, *Evaluating Authentic Assessment*, is particularly relevant to the aims of the series, since it draws together the collective experience of a number of leading British researchers in the field of educational assessment. Draft versions of the chapters in this volume were originally presented in three different symposia at the 1993 American Educational Research

Association Annual Conference in Atlanta, Georgia. Together they provide an overview of issues, problems and empirical evidence from a variety of developments in England and Wales including public examinations at school-leaving age (the General Certificate of Secondary Education (GCSE)), National Curriculum assessment, and post-compulsory National Vocational Qualifications (NVQs). The contributors have long experience of developing and evaluating new approaches to assessment in the UK and the strength of the volume, both for a British and an international audience, is that it takes debate beyond the particular strengths and weaknesses of individual initiatives and offers a broader insight into the problems and possibilities inherent in new approaches, and in particular the difficulties of moving from good intentions to good practice.

Another strength of the volume is that the contributors are also very aware of the political context in which change is taking place, and the impact which this has on 'educational' developments. Such impact is often ignored or even condemned in some educational accounts of change, but the contributors to this volume, with an eye on the evaluation of policy as well as practice, treat the political context as integral to the process of change and look to the costs, benefits and political trade-offs which inevitably accompany change in such a highly sensitive area of educational and indeed social policy. The contributors are also united in their analysis that too mechanistic a view of policy development and implementation will lead to disappointment. Changes in assessment alone will not improve schools; they must be part of a wider package of curriculum and professional development if they are to be properly understood and engaged with in individual schools and classrooms.

Harry Torrance

ACKNOWLEDGEMENTS

The work reported in this book draws on empirical research conducted over a number of years and funded by a variety of sponsors. Acknowledgement of individual sponsors is made in each chapter as appropriate. However, it is also appropriate to mention that the editor and contributors have been able to meet (along with other researchers) on a regular basis under the auspices of the Nuffield Assessment Seminar, supported by the Nuffield Foundation. This seminar has brought together individuals from a variety of disciplinary and professional backgrounds working in the field of assessment, to discuss issues of current concern, and the book can be seen as an indirect outcome of such discussions.

The editor would also like to acknowledge the help of Margaret Ralph in editing material supplied by contributors on disk.

Finally, the editor would like to acknowledge the interest and support of John Skelton in the production of this book and the series of which it is part.

INTRODUCTION

Harry Torrance

'Authentic assessment' is a generic term which is gaining international currency to describe a range of new approaches to assessment. The basic implication of the term seems to be that the assessment tasks designed for students should be more practical, realistic and challenging than what one might call 'traditional' paper-and-pencil tests. The term 'performance assessment' is also quite widely used to describe such new approaches. In the United Kingdom 'coursework assessment' or 'school-based assessment' has generally been taken to describe such new methods, though of course traditional paper-and-pencil tests can be, and often still are, set or administered by teachers in schools.

New approaches to assessment have emerged in a number of countries over the last several years, out of a variety of overlapping debates about the purposes and methods of assessment, and about its impact on the process of teaching and learning. These debates derive from a number of intellectual and professional perspectives. They are also taking place in the context of intense political debate about the accountability of education services (and school systems in particular) and in what ways changes in assessment practices and procedures can contribute to educational reform and raising 'standards'.

Thus arguments over the need to develop and implement much more challenging curricular programmes inevitably involve discussion over how they should be assessed, from the point of view both of assessment validity, and of not inhibiting such curriculum change. In the UK, for example, more coursework assessment and practical assessment has been implemented over recent years in the new General Certificate of Secondary Education (GCSE) as curriculum change has involved the use of more practical work in science and technology, more emphasis on oral communication in English and foreign languages, more local fieldwork studies in history and geography, and so forth. The new educational objectives of planning, carrying out and writing up extended tasks, or of speaking and listening effectively, could not be validly tested by one-off paper-and-pencil tests – hence the technical need to develop and use new methods of assessment to be conducted over a period of time within the school. At one and the same time it is well recognized that traditional testing formats will inhibit such curriculum change, and thus there are also good curriculum development arguments for implementing assessment change alongside curriculum change.

More recently, however, this coincidence of interest between assessment agencies and curriculum developers has been given a new twist by arguments suggesting that changes in assessment might come *first*, and lead (or even 'drive') the curriculum in desirable directions – broaden the scope of the assessment system and increase the complexity and the demands of the tasks involved, and you will broaden the curriculum and raise the standard of teaching. Thus it is argued that traditional paper-and-pencil tests – particularly multiple choice tests – can have a narrowing effect on the curriculum, in terms both of curriculum content and of teaching methods employed, and that such an approach to learning can result in children coming to know certain things without understanding them and without being able to generalize from specific examples to similar problems in different contexts. Worse still, repeated failure can lead to increased truancy and drop-out. In parallel with such criticisms, it is further argued that for the situation to be improved assessment must take account of higher-order skills and competencies such as problem-solving, investigation and analysis, and thus must involve far more 'authentic' or realistic tasks than have traditionally been employed in the field. In turn, these new authentic assessments will lead to improved teaching and learning in schools as teachers adopt their classroom and laboratory practices to ensure that their students succeed at the new tasks (ILEA 1984; Murphy and Torrance 1988; Nickerson 1989; Cole 1990; Gifford and O'Connor 1992).

In tandem with such debates about the relationship of assessment to curriculum change there has also been considerable interest in the relationship of assessment to learning and particularly the role that assessment might play in the promotion of learning – formative assessment. Of course, diagnostic assessment has a long history, particularly in the field of special education – that is, using tests to assess student progress for purposes of guidance and perhaps to identify particular learning difficulties. Also it has long been recognized, as noted above, that assessment can have a *negative* impact on learning. However, at least some versions of formative assessment, usually associated with a constructivist perspective on the process of learning, would appear to be taking a more positive, dynamic and forward-looking approach to the relationship between assessment, teaching and learning, and thus to establish, not so much what students have learned, or have not learned, but what they *might* learn in the immediate future with appropriate help from a teacher or peer (Brown and Ferrara 1985; Brown *et al.* 1992; Torrance 1993a). Developments in this field have often been more research-orientated and distanced from policy-making than interventions in formal testing or examining procedures, but they clearly form part of an overall constellation of educational interest in new forms of assessment, and in the UK in particular have been taken on board in certain policy-making arenas (Broadfoot *et al.* 1988; Task Group on Assessment and Testing (TGAT) 1988).

Educational change does not take place in a social or political vacuum, of course, and much of the impetus for change in assessment has come from political interest in rendering schools more accountable and using testing to raise standards. However, just as educational interests differ, so do political interests, and they have found expression in a variety of different approaches to using assessment in educational reform. Thus over twenty years ago governments on both sides of the Atlantic set up national monitoring programmes to sample educational achievement and attempt to measure whether or not standards were rising or falling – the American National Assessment of Educational Performance (NAEP) and the British Assessment of Performance Unit (APU). However, because national monitoring is based on sampling it cannot directly influence each and every classroom, and subsequently programmes of minimum competency testing and 'measurement-driven instruction' in the United States, and now National Curriculum assessment in the UK, have been introduced to try to impact directly on what is taught in schools and how it is taught. The overlap of interest with those educationists who have similarly been arguing that measurement can and should 'drive' instruction (for example, Popham 1987) is clear enough, though most educational arguments centre around the issues outlined above and involve a call for the use of more demanding 'authentic' assessments in such programmes rather than even more multiple-choice testing (Shepard 1991; Office of Technology Assessment 1992; Resnick and Resnick 1992).

The political picture is further complicated by the use to which assessment *results* can be put in league tables of school performance. This is particularly the case at the present time in the UK as the government has introduced a 'market system' into publicly provided and funded schooling. Thus schools are being given increasing control over their own budgets (moving control away from local education authorities – i.e. school districts) at the same time as parents can exercise some choice over school placement (within available school capacity) and also at the same time as league tables of test and examination results are being produced and published by the government. The pressure on schools to maximize test results is clear, though at what cost to 'real' education is a matter of debate. The main implication for the discussion here, however, is that the political need for simple, quick tests which can produce comparable results across very large groups of students, means that the pressure to return to paper-and-pencil tests is enormous, and this is an issue that is raised in a number of contributions to this volume.

Before moving on briefly to review each contribution, and especially for the benefit of an international audience, it is probably worthwhile outlining the current 'state of play' with regard to the particular developments to which the contributions refer. The

GCSE was created out of the merger of the General Certificate of Education (GCE) O level and the Certificate of Secondary Education (CSE). Broadly speaking, GCE was intended for the top 20% of the ability range and was very much a 'traditional' subject-based academic examination; CSE was intended for the next 40% of the ability range, and, while it included more innovative examination subjects and formats, remained for the most part a 'pale imitation' of O level. GCSE was finally launched as a single examination system in 1986, with its first candidates examined in 1988, to rationalize the dual system. Its launch provided the opportunity for considerable curriculum and assessment change so that far more practical and project-based assessment was included than in O level or CSE.

The National Certificate of Vocational Qualifications is attempting to rationalize a large number of disparate post-compulsory (16+) vocational qualifications. It is aimed at post-compulsory school and college students, and also at employees in training. It has introduced a performance-based form of post-compulsory curriculum and assessment; and teaching, learning and assessment are now intended to be accomplished 'on the job' or in highly practical simulations or practical placements.

National Curriculum assessment is hardest of all to summarize, since it has been constantly changing since first introduced by the Education Reform Act and the TGAT Report in 1988. Originally the National Curriculum comprised a 'core' of English, maths and science, with a 'foundation' of technology, history, geography, art, music, physical education and a modern foreign language from 11+. Pupils were to be assessed in all subjects, with reporting in terms of National Curriculum 'levels' at the end of each 'Key Stage' of the curriculum (ages 7, 11, 14 and 16). National Curriculum levels were to run from 1 to 10, with the 'average' pupil being expected to progress by one level every two years from age 5 to 16. These levels were to be determined by students' achievement in the 'Attainment Targets' which were to be prescribed by Working Groups in each subject.

The curriculum was introduced simultaneously across Key Stages but assessment was introduced into Key Stage 1 first, and it is still most developed at Key Stage 1 (ages 5–7). Assessment was to be conducted by a combination of teacher assessment (TA) of students' performance in class and Standard Assessment Tasks

(SATs). Initially, lengthy and complex tasks were designed for Key Stage 1 SATs but these have been progressively narrowed towards paper-and-pencil tests (as Broadfoot, McCallum *et al.* and Gipps discuss in this volume; cf. also Torrance 1991a). Similar developments have occurred at Key Stages 2 and 3, but these developments were still only at a pilot stage in 1993. Latterly, because of immense teacher resistance, including a widespread boycott of assessment in 1993, a government report has recommended 'slimming down' the National Curriculum and its attendant assessment programme, so that each subject will include far less prescribed material and SATs (now known as Standard Tests) will be used only in the 'core' subjects (Dearing 1994). The problems of implementing such a demanding assessment programme, and the implications of narrowing it down, are the specific focus of Chapters 1, 3 and 5.

In Chapter 1 Patricia Broadfoot examines the emerging practice of authentic or performance assessment as it is manifest in a variety of national initiatives, before going on to highlight some particular problems in the attempt to implement more valid approaches to assessment in the SATs for the National Curriculum assessment programme in England and Wales. The chapter draws on research on the introduction of the National Curriculum which Broadfoot conducted with others. Problems of implementation arose as a result of the attempt to operationalize complex assessment tasks on a national scale at classroom level. In particular, Broadfoot examines the problems inherent in trying to operationalize complicated tasks in a 'standard' fashion with very young children and little in the way of prior training for teachers.

In Chapter 2 Harry Torrance examines the aspiration for authentic assessment to improve teaching. The chapter addresses the ways in which teachers become involved in developments in assessment and interpret and mediate developments at classroom level. The chapter draws on evidence from teacher involvement in coursework assessment in GCSE, graded testing, Records of Achievement and National Curriculum assessment, and demonstrates that if changes in assessment are implemented with little or no explanation they will be interpreted from a 'testing' rather than a 'teaching' perspective and many of the intended curricular and pedagogical benefits of such change will not be realized.

Chapter 3 reports some findings from a research project looking specifically at National Curriculum assessment in primary schools.

Bet McCallum, Caroline Gipps, Shelley McAlister and Margaret Brown explore teachers' interpretations and practice of TA at Key Stage 1. This complements the discussion of SATs in Chapter 1. The chapter provides further detailed evidence about the variety of ways in which policy is interpreted and mediated at classroom level. It goes on to construct a typology of teachers' approaches to teacher assessment which demonstrates how emerging assessment practices are linked to teachers' views of how children learn.

Chapter 4, by Alison Wolf, reports on the development of authentic assessment in the post-compulsory vocational education sector. Here the logic of performance assessment has been extended by its proponents to insist on all assessments being made under realistic performance conditions – preferably 'on-the-job' – and all new vocational courses being written in terms of directly assessable practical competences. The chapter draws attention to the proliferation of assessment under these conditions and stresses the need for collaborative assessor 'networks' to underpin claims for reliability and comparability. However, the post-compulsory sector is also becoming increasingly competitive, with colleges competing with other colleges and also private training agencies for students, and Wolf suggests that this runs counter to the need for collaboration when determining and securing comparable assessment standards.

Caroline Gipps, in Chapter 5, raises similar issues of manageability and reliability. She draws further on her research team's empirical work, but in this chapter to address issues of the reliability and comparability of results, rather than impact at classroom level. The chapter explores the variability of administration and marking within schools, as well as across schools, along with problems of managing authentic assessment in large groups. Gipps confirms Wolf's judgement that supportive 'moderation' networks, discussing criteria and evidence, can improve consistency.

In Chapter 6 Hilary Radnor and Ken Shaw follow up this brief discussion of moderation by reviewing the problems and possibilities of moderation and outlining one particular approach taken in a specific development project. The chapter stresses that for moderation to have most effect it should be seen as an integral part of an overall approach to course planning and quality control, thus also contributing to teachers' professional development. Moderation should not simply focus on the consistency of final results.

Finally, in Chapter 7 Harry Torrance reviews the emerging international use of assessment in educational reform. The chapter outlines the variety of ways in which the role of assessment in educational reform is being conceptualized and practised and draws attention to the problems and possibilities inherent in different approaches. He draws on the evidence reported in previous chapters to caution against assuming too mechanistic a relationship between assessment and teaching.

1

PERFORMANCE ASSESSMENT IN PERSPECTIVE: INTERNATIONAL TRENDS AND CURRENT ENGLISH EXPERIENCE

Patricia Broadfoot

Introduction: a changing assessment agenda

The development of performance assessment techniques is an increasingly characteristic feature of the education systems of the developed world. The urgent need to promote the learning of skills and competences *that cannot be tested by more traditional techniques*, and to report on these, lies behind a range of related developments in international assessment and reporting practice.

Historically, the practice of educational assessment has been largely driven by a perceived need to *measure* individual intellectual capacity. When educational assessment first began to be widely used in the nineteenth century, this was in response to the institution of mass educational provision and the associated need to provide a 'ladder of opportunity' into the expanding industrial economies of that era. The pressing need to find mechanisms of selection that would be both socially acceptable and identify the 'best' candidates, led to a premium being put on assessment techniques that appeared to be fair and objective, that had high levels of reliability.

In such a 'high stakes' environment in which, to a very significant extent, test results determined life chances, it was inevitable that there should be an overwhelming emphasis on reliability so that the assessment might be seen to operate fairly and consistently. The question of validity – whether the test does indeed measure what it is intended to measure – has arguably been subordinated to the overwhelming need for comparability of results. The pre-occupation with reliability has, in turn, tended to lead to a concentration on that which is more readily measurable – such as knowledge and understanding and a relative, if not absolute, neglect of higher-level intellectual skills, of personal and social competences and attitudes (Wilson, 1992).

The prevailing assessment culture is still steeped in these pre-occupations despite the fact that the social imperatives for assessment today are very different from those of a century ago. Curriculum goals have changed and broadened. There is a higher priority on encouraging people to continue their education rather than on excluding them. Above all, there is an urgent need for education systems to train people who will have the appropriate range of skills and attitudes to be capable of undertaking a variety of work roles in a climate of rapid technological change. Problem-solving ability, personal effectiveness, thinking skills and willingness to accept change are typical of the general competencies straddling cognitive and affective domains that are now being sought in young people. To the extent that the assessment industry falls short of matching these new educational priorities with appropriate new techniques, so it will also inhibit the pursuit of such new educational goals.

As a growing international awareness of the need for change in assessment priorities is leading to a range of significant initiatives, so the problems of bringing about such a major change in the way we think about assessment are becoming increasingly apparent. At the heart of the problems is the *Zeitgeist* of a previous age – a set of unquestioned assumptions concerning assessment priorities which in turn inform judgements concerning the merits of particular techniques. As Nisbet (1992) suggests:

> Public and professional attitudes to assessment in education constitute an 'assessment culture' which, like other cultures,

rests on a common set of assumptions and beliefs, and depends on familiarity and long established practices. It is not surprising that the process of change is slow and difficult.

In what follows I explore, first, some of the *policy issues* in performance assessment. The aim will be to examine the rationale for performance assessment as it is embodied in different national initiatives and, in so doing, to classify the nature and scale of the changes currently taking place. The second part of the chapter focuses more directly on some of the technical issues in performance assessment as these have been identified in the particular example of National Curriculum assessment in England and Wales.

Policy issues in performance assessment

One of the difficulties inherent in any attempt to examine issues concerning performance assessment is the problem of precise definition and boundaries. In particular, I shall argue here that many of the technical problems which we are beginning to identify concerning performance assessment are caused by its inappropriate use, rather than by shortcomings in the approach *per se*. Or, to put it another way, while it may prove possible in the longer term to develop performance assessments which are sufficiently reliable to bear the weight of 'high stakes' selection decisions for individual careers and/or 'high stakes' institutional judgements, it remains doubtful whether it is possible to design performance assessments of this kind which are also useful for diagnostic and formative purposes. It may be, as Stiggins (1992) suggests, that large-scale assessment programmes cannot meet teachers' very different assessment needs.

Evidence that this may be so is increasingly being provided by the attempts of a number of different countries to increase the element of performance assessment within traditional certificate examinations and by the much more novel and radical initiatives aimed at both monitoring and indeed raising national standards of achievement by the assiduous use of assessment. The rationale for both these developments is rooted in the changing assessment culture referred to above which prioritizes the promotion of higher and more appropriate learning outcomes rather than the search for the most accurate ways of measuring these.

International comparisons provide for a more detailed definition of the elements of this new culture as follows:

1 An increasing emphasis on formative, learning-integrated assessment throughout the process of education.
2 A commitment to raising the level of teacher understanding and of expertise in assessment procedures associated with the devolution of responsibility for quality assurance in the certification process.
3 An increasing emphasis on validity in the assessment process which allows the full range of curriculum objectives including cognitive, psychomotor and even affective domains of learning to be addressed by the use of a wider range of more 'authentic' techniques for gathering evidence of learning outcomes.
4 An increasing emphasis on describing learning outcomes in terms of particular standards achieved – often associated with the pre-specification of such outcomes in a way that reflects the integration of curriculum and assessment planning.
5 An increasing emphasis on using the assessment of individual pupils' learning outcomes as an indicator of the quality of educational provision, whether this be at the level of the individual classroom, the institution, the state, the nation or for international comparisons.

Some examples from Australia are cited here since they are indicative of these trends; then some brief comparative comments are offered on some of the initiatives in a number of other countries before I deal with the experience of National Curriculum assessment in England and Wales in detail.

Australia

Concern to monitor standards on a national basis in Australia, as well as in individual states, is reflected in the Australasian Cooperative Assessment Programme which is involved in devising national subject profiles for mathematics and literacy/English. The origins of this initiative are described in the report of the Working Party on Basic Skills and Program Evaluation of the Australian Education Council 1989 as follows:

The development of national subject profiles must be closely linked with national curriculum development. It would then be possible to develop a framework comprising a sequence of levels through which students progress . . . Levels could be established for each major component of a subject. For example, literacy could be thought of as a composite of reading, writing, listening and speaking, each with its own sequence of levels . . . The levels could be defined by a set of *assessment tasks* which could be standardised and widely publicised among schools and the community generally. These tasks could include pencil and paper tests, observation of student performance against set criteria, assignments, etc. Various systems may have a preference for various modes of assessment.

The crucial point to note here is that standardization of the assessments is not to be the product of common tasks but is rather to be achieved by the provision of extensive illustrative material which teachers can use as a basis for judging their own students' performance.

Individual states have also taken their own initiatives in this respect. In Western Australia, for example, a Monitoring Standards in Education Program has produced benchmarks for English and mathematics and has developed assessment tasks to assess the performance of students in Years 3, 7 and 10. These assessments show system-wide performance but *not* individual, school or area-based results. The same materials can also be used by teachers, however, as part of their normal classroom assessment or as part of school development planning. The approach is illustrated in Appendices 1.1 and 1.2 (from *Monitoring Standards in Education*, Ministry of Education, Western Australia, 1991).

The approach of the Western Australian MSE is different from the approach taken in the Victorian and NSW testing programs in that it begins with the attempt to make explicit the levels of performance expected of students in Years 3, 7 and 10. In this sense, the 'benchmarks' resemble the 'attainment targets' of the English National Curriculum. In contrast, the Victorian and NSW programs estimate and report levels of student achievement without reference to pre-specified standards. Any judgements about minimum acceptable levels of performance are likely to be made only after test results are available.

A second feature of the MSE project is that it is designed to make standard assessment tasks available to teachers for their own monitoring purposes. Assessment tasks used as part of the 1990 testing will be made available free-of-charge to all government schools in Western Australia in Term 4, 1990. Because these tasks will have been used with a sample of WA schools, teachers using them will be able to compare the performances of their own students with results for the state.

In common with NSW and Victoria, the WA Monitoring Standards in Education program uses item response theory (IRT) as the basis for defining levels of achievement within each of a number of subject profile components.

(Masters 1990)

The assumption behind this approach is that performance assessment can best be made by a combination of verbal descriptions of achievement levels with examples of the kinds of task and behaviour that illustrate those levels. Sadler (1987) argues that

verbal descriptions, on the one hand, have a significant role to play in drawing attention to the particular criteria that are salient at different points on a grading scale. They therefore provide valuable keys into complex evaluative frameworks. But because of the variable interpretation of terms, *verbal statements need concrete referents*. The respective strengths of exemplars on the one hand and verbal descriptions on the other suggest the possibility of specifying standards efficiently by a combination of the two.

A slightly different approach to performance assessment which relies more heavily on observation in a number of routine classroom situations than on specially organized assessment events is illustrated by the Victorian literacy profiles, as Figure 1.1 shows. This is essentially a way of structuring teachers' observations within a hierarchical set of benchmarks to make explicit the professional monitoring of individual children's progress that is an integral part of teaching.

LITERACY PROFILE

SCHOOL ___*EASTERN PRIMARY*___ CLASS _*PREP.*_   YEAR: 19 ?

NAME ___*l. .. V_ .. ..*___ TERM   CONTEXT OF OBSERVATION   COMMENTS

READING BAND   A   ☐

Concepts about Print ☐——
Holds book the right way up.
Turns pages from the front to the back.
On request, indicates the beginning and end of sentences.
Distinguishes between upper and lower case letters.
Indicates the start and end of books.
Reading Strategies ☐——
Locates words, lines, spaces, letters.
Refers to letters by name.
Locates own name and other familiar words in a short text.
Identifies known, familiar words in other contexts.
Responses ☑——
Responds to literature (smiles, claps, listens intently)
Joins in familiar stories.
Interest and Attitudes ☑——
Shows preference for particular books.
Chooses books as a free time activity

'helper' at shared reading time.

| shared. reading library

| quiet rdg time

borrows 9 takes books home

Figure 1.1 Literacy profile
Source: Ministry of Education, Victoria, *Literacy Profiles Handbook*, 1990

This use of benchmarks and verbal descriptions as the basis for performance assessment is being developed in many other countries as well. A very similar approach is to be found in the Toronto 'benchmark' Standards of Student Achievement in Canada, as Appendix 1.3 illustrates. In this initiative, empirically derived standards are used to provide level descriptors in a number of set tasks in key curriculum areas. Teachers use the task to standardize their reporting of student achievement to gauge how well their students are doing.

In New Zealand, the 1990 Tomorrow's Standards Report recommended the use of 'standard assessment tasks' to sample learning outcomes for students of 8 and 12 years of age on a four-year cycle (Crooks 1993). The recently launched 'Achievement Initiative' is designed to meet this need by providing teachers with specially developed tasks on which to base their classroom assessment.

United States

The United States provides extensive evidence for the existence of a changing assessment agenda. For example, in California the new state-wide student assessment program takes the ambitious view that performance assessment which includes asking students to speak, research, create and experiment as well as write, can be a basis for state-wide testing. According to Bill Honig, California's former State Superintendent of Public Instruction:

> The assumption was that a subjective grading process was appropriate for classroom assessment, but not for public accountability. But we can and must standardize these more valid assessments – it's either that or live with the results of narrow assessment and poor accountability.

In addition to the use of open-ended problems, enhanced multiple-choice questions and investigations, portfolios are also a significant development. Such a planned selection of students' work collected from work done throughout the school year not only allows teachers, parents and others to see the developing pattern in students' learning and across a wide range of knowledge and skills, it also allows students to be active in the assessment process, which will help to enhance their metacognitive strategies. Similar initiatives are taking place in many other states, including Vermont, Michigan, Connecticut and Maine (Koretz *et al.* 1992).

The United Kingdom

The United Kingdom provides one of the starkest illustrations of the various policy issues surrounding the introduction of performance assessment in the context of the rather different strategies being employed to provide for national assessment in England and Wales, Scotland and Northern Ireland (Broadfoot *et al.* 1992).

In England and Wales the 1988 Education Reform Act introduced, for the first time, a national curriculum for Years 1–10 with defined attainment targets and regular assessment of students against these targets by both continuous teacher assessment (TA) and Standard Assessment Tasks (SATs), the latter to be administered at the end of each of four 'Key Stages' and to be expressed in terms of ten hierarchical levels. The rationale for this assessment was provided by the Task Group on Assessment and Testing (TGAT) whose 1988 report identified four purposes for national assessment: diagnostic, formative, summative and evaluative.

In Northern Ireland, by contrast, the aim is to use a combination of Common Assessment Instruments (CAIs), External Assessment Resources (EARs) and continuous teacher assessment. EARs involve the provision of resources for teachers to use as part of the normal teaching–learning situation but which are specifically arranged and targeted at particular levels of achievement to provide assessment information. In a letter to the Chairman of the Northern Ireland School Examinations and Assessment Council (NISEAC) dated 27 February 1991, Lord Belstead wrote that 'the external assessment resources . . . should produce valuable information for teachers which will help them plan their work with each child, and moreover should be of significant assistance in their evaluation of their teaching strategies'. The CAIs are broadly similar to the SATs used in England and Wales which are described in more detail later in this chapter. Like the SATs, they will become progressively more like conventional tests as students increase in age (NISEAC, 1992).

In Scotland, performance assessment has also been introduced in response to government concerns to improve the assessment and reporting of student learning.

> The guidelines on assessment (SOED 1991) provide a theoretical framework for practice in schools which is supported by specific arrangements for the testing of children in P4 and P7 across three curricular areas – reading, writing and mathematics. In the pilot round (1991) and first reported period (1992) of National Testing, the intention was that pupils at the above stages would be tested within specified periods of the school session. Test material is from the 'bank' of units built up and held in the Primary Assessment Unit (PAU) of the Scottish Examination Board (SEB). Scrutiny of such units across the five attainment levels (A–E) reveals in the main, an attractive range of assessment materials which are criterion – rather than norm – referenced.'
>
> (Thomson and Ward 1992)

There was a widespread parental boycott of the tests of 7-year-olds in Scotland. Parents feared too much pressure on children with very little benefit to children, teachers or parents.

In consequence, these arrangements have now been changed. As from November 1992 teachers will have a catalogue of assessment resources and can administer their chosen tasks whenever they feel an individual pupil is ready. It remains to be seen if this more individualized approach to assessment is manageable in the context of a large class of children, but whatever the outcome, events in Scotland underline the crucial policy point in relation to performance assessment that where external testing for summative or evaluative purposes is unacceptable *in principle*, increasing the validity of the assessment will be unlikely to change this. In this respect it might be said that Scottish parents' expectations of assessment derived from their experience of a previous culture of assessment, and that they were not prepared to give novel instruments the benefit of the doubt.

France

The opposite point is, interestingly enough, made in France, where comprehensive national assessment has been introduced for explicitly formative purposes. Teachers are required to administer centrally devised tests to their students at the *beginning* of certain 'key stages' – and to use the information so generated as the basis for a more individualized pedagogy (Broadfoot 1992). Unfortunately, however, because the assessments are not 'integral' either to teachers' ideology or to their classroom practice, neither of which is typically informed by a child-centred perspective, it is proving difficult for teachers to make effective use of the information so generated (Pluvinage 1992).

Problems in implementing performance assessment with young children

Having briefly reviewed some of the ways in which performance assessment has been incorporated into recent assessment policy initiatives in different countries, it is appropriate to explore in more depth some of the technical problems that have characterized these attempts. In what follows, I draw on the results of a project sponsored by the Economic and Social Research Council which is monitoring the impact of the National Curriculum and its assessment procedures on primary schools, teachers and children. The data were gathered during the 1991 and 1992 SAT administration using a combination of classroom observation and interviews with teachers and pupils in nine classrooms from across England. Data were also gathered from interviews and questionnaires with teachers from a larger nationally representative sample of 48 schools.

It is appropriate to use the particular assessment initiative of SATs at Key Stage 1 (7-year-olds) for close analysis because the tasks set have, from the outset, been intended to represent best practice in performance assessment. Children have been asked to undertake tasks which are open-ended, engrossing and stimulating, designed to enable them to demonstrate the whole range of skills embodied in a particular Attainment Target. That this was generally achieved is borne out by observational data which recorded consistently high levels of student interest and enthusiasm and by interview data in which students said how much they had enjoyed the tasks.

The SAT example to be focused on here is a fairly conventional maths exercise which was chosen for study because it was one of the more standardized SATs and therefore should have had fewer problems of reliability (Appendix 1.4). While the task was designed to be used with large groups, typically teachers assessed the children in small groups with the rest of the class being taken by a colleague or teaching aide, although sometimes such support was not available. Regardless of how they were organized, the administration of the SATs evoked a range of concerns among teachers. These included constraints on normal classroom practice; whether a common stimulus to perform was being provided; whether children who were aware of being tested were underperforming because of anxiety; whether children who did *not* know they were being assessed were therefore also underperforming; and whether teachers were being broadly consistent with different groups of children and in relation to each other in the amount of help being given.

The changes in normal classroom style brought about by the requirements of SATs were much in evidence to the research team, especially teachers not being able to intervene in a testing situation in order to promote learning. Teachers felt they could not engage in their normal classroom behaviour of, for example, listening and showing, when a child intervened into a conversation or activity in some way. Though the official position regarding SATs has, from the outset, been that the SAT activities can be woven into a teacher's half-term theme so that they can constitute learning experiences in themselves, this contradicts the requirements of the test process that teachers must avoid giving children direct help and 'asking questions that lead the child to the correct response'. Teachers found this an unnatural way of working and felt the children could not understand the change in their practice, as our fieldnotes indicate:

> A teacher remarked (St Bede's, 1991): I really find it so frustrating being unable to help them when they don't understand.
>
> At another school the teacher had to rebuke 2 children, Adam and Tracy, who have begun to discuss their work: 'Adam, Tracy, if I have to tell you not to talk again, I may get angry.' Which produced in the children a puzzled and slightly hurt reaction at this strange departure from normal classroom practice.

Teachers disliked having to reverse the pattern of co-operative, collaborative work in their classrooms:

> Another teacher was heard to say: No, go away Paul. I don't want you to see this.
>
> Later she commented: He looked at me as if I'd gone mad.

Torrance (1991a) similarly reports that teachers in consequence often felt deskilled because pre-specified tasks and the observation of pre-specified outcomes is fundamentally against the logic of the infant classroom. Pupils inevitably noticed the change in the teacher's role.

Other unorthodox features of teachers' classroom practice during SATs may be identified as giving covert messages to children that the activity was not routine even if the children did not know, as many children appeared not to know, especially in 1991, that they were being tested. Indeed, depending on the school, many children appeared to lack the conceptual vocabulary to understand what testing is. For example, one teacher working in a busy classroom differentiated her interaction with the SAT children quite clearly by lowering her voice, a cue that this was not 'normal' work.

Unusual seating arrangements – three to a table usually occupied by six children, for example, to prevent collaboration – were other features which not only tended to inhibit teachers' attempts to present SATs as just one of a number of ongoing classroom activities, but also appeared to cause stress to both teachers and pupils to the extent that they represented an imposition of different modes of classroom interaction.

How standardized were the SATs themselves?

Variability in the organization in which SATs took place meant that children were given different contexts in which to show their level of achievement. In addition to these variations, our data identify a range of sources of variability within the operation of the task itself which are also likely to have affected children's ability to demonstrate their achievement.

Variability in teacher stimulus

Stage in a given SAT

One whole range of variables clusters around the notion of possible reactions to the experience of testing. One obvious source of potential significance concerns who conducts the tests and the stage reached in the SAT process. Our fieldnotes charted a consistent pattern in relation to subsequent groups of pupils undertaking the same SAT. Typically, this starts with a relative lack of confidence on the part of the teacher caused by lack of familiarity, rising to a peak of performance on the second or third application of a given SAT, when the teacher was sufficiently confident and at ease with a particular SAT task to be able to present it in the most positive way for pupils. In contrast, we documented teachers' flagging enthusiasm and boredom as they commenced the same task, in some cases, for the ninth time, and found themselves unable to stimulate the children to perform in the same way as earlier groups because of this.

It is not without significance either that the children were thought likely to respond differently to someone they know conducting the SATs than to a stranger or other teacher. Teachers were so sensitive to this issue that in one case in 1991 a teacher came back, unpaid, from maternity leave to undertake SATs because

> (Mrs AR, Kenwood School): I feel the children need to do SATs with someone who knows them really well.

Whether testing is made explicit

Perhaps the most significant issue in this respect, however, is whether or not the teacher made the reality of testing explicit to the children and what consequences this decision may have had. In some cases the SAT was presented as a game, in others as a learning activity, and in a few as a test. In many classrooms, if you did not know what was going on, you would not have realized that some children were involved in an assessment activity.

In one classroom in 1992 the teacher was so concerned about the impact of the Maths 3 SAT in particular, involving the pressure of both timing and clearly right or wrong answers, that she was prepared to undertake testing the children on a one-to-one basis in a class of 30, even though this caused major administrative problems. Indeed, it is an illustration of the strength of the teacher's commitment to protect the children from anxiety and from a feeling of failure that she was prepared to engage in a lengthy period in which there was relatively little teaching for the rest of the class in order to provide this.

It was particularly noticeable in the more explicit testing materials of 1992 that the unambiguous nature of some of the SATs, notably the maths test, produced a greater tension and anxiety in the children and a greater awareness of failure which some teachers took great pains to avoid. This was done by a variety of subterfuges – for example, in one school:

> All of the group have finished Level 2. Teacher says: 'Right, books away.'
> To the others: 'Raymond finished this on Friday so we'll let him go back to class now.'
> It was explained later that this was the exit point from the test for Raymond, disguised as the rest move on to attempt Level 3, to avoid hurting his feelings.
> In this same school, the teacher presented another SAT as a game:

'Charles got 5, Raymond got 5, and Graham got 6, so Graham is champion.

OK, mighty Graham, go back to class and tell Mrs P that you are the champion at these. Ten housepoints for you.'

(Fieldnotes, St Anne's School)

How the SATs were presented

On almost all occasions when SATs were observed, activities were presented as fun or as part of normal classroom life, which both observation and later interviews with children suggested were accepted as such. In 1991, although 32% of teachers in our sample reported that some children showed signs of stress, most reported no special reaction (59%) and 63% of the teachers who responded suggested that the children experienced, rather, considerable enjoyment in doing the SATs. Occasionally, children demonstrated awareness of some element of assessment in the activities in such responses as:

Maybe she wanted to test us out in those things.

or

To see if we're good at it.

More often, children happily admitted that they had no idea why they had been asked to carry out the activities.

I don't know. She said, 'Four of you will be with me.' I don't know why.

They seemed to accept this, whether they described the tasks with enthusiasm:

It was fun. I really liked it.

or indifference:

A bit boring, but quite nice.

Teachers' strategies for avoiding stress in children included making no overt reference to, or demonstration of, assessment in their presence. Children were not usually dismissed from a group if they were clearly finding the task too difficult but were allowed to continue with teacher assistance which meant that they would not be considered to have reached the level on which they worked.

Sometimes they were told that they had worked extremely well but that they looked tired and 'could leave this work for now'. So much so that one teacher even wondered whether her children's relaxed attitude to the SATs was conducive to their producing the best work of which they were capable or whether some awareness of being tested might have lent an edge to their performance. The rather unorthodox implementation of the Maths 3 SATs in one school in 1992 bears out this argument to some extent:

> The teacher says: 'We're going to start off nice and easy so Steven won't get his worried face, and Rebecca won't get her frown.' (Funny expressions on his face) 'To help you, you'll have these sheets.'
>
> He reads out: '4 + 2 Ugh! (pulls a face) 2 + 3 Ugh! They're very easy. As soon as you've finished, turn over your paper and take out your puzzle book. You won't need to look at anyone else's because they're *so* easy. Don't worry if you get left behind. It's only a bit of fun and we'll have another competition later. So, remember the rules: no looking at anyone else's, no showing anyone else. When you've finished I'll come round and give team points.'
>
> 'We've all got to start together to make it fair, so put your name on it, but don't start yet. To help you, you can use number trail or counters. It's only a bit of fun to make up some points.'
>
> 'When I count 3 you can start – no-one must see yours. Otherwise it won't be a fair competition. Don't forget the counters if you need them.'
>
> (In the context of a competition or a game, not being allowed to co-operate seems acceptable to the children, even though it's not the way they normally work.)
>
> He goes round the tables: 'I told you they were easy. Don't forget the top are take-aways and the bottom adds.'
>
> (Carla has already finished and taken out her puzzle.)
>
> 'Jason, ssh! Good girl. She's got her paper turned over so I know she's finished. Let's see which table comes first. If it were Rainbow Table it would be good because there's someone from every team on their table.'

'Carla is finished and Heather and Clare and Steven. OK, Yellow Team is finished and that's 20 points to them.'

(Continuing the competition theme.)

'Which team will be next? Oh, yes, we're only waiting for Michael on that table now.'

Says to Steven: 'Don't forget, the ones on the bottom are take-aways, *not* add-ups.'

'How are we doing now? A couple more minutes then, there'll be a chance to win some more points with another game.'

'One more to go – will Red Team get third? No, it's Blue Team who are finished. Well done, Blue Team. Ten more points for Blue Team.'

'All right, close your puzzle books. Now, the next one you'll have to be really speedy so switch your brains on.'

'Now, there are some silly shapes here. (Holds up fruits and shows whole class – points out and names each fruit.) Not to worry about them, they're just a bit of fun to put the answers in. I'm only going to give you 5 seconds for each answer. Don't worry if you miss out, just jump on to the next one. The apples and oranges are just a funny space to put the answer in. Instead of a box, you've got an apple to put the answer in.'

(Gives out sheets)

Gives an example of how to do it: 'Let's think of an easy sum and we'll all write it down. 2 + 1 – can you write number 3 in the apple shape in the black box. Now, when I ask you another sum, you write the answer in the orange shape. That's all you have to do. Go down the black box side. If you like, you can put your finger on the orange so you know what to write next.'

(Shows cards with sums and numbers. Holds card with number 1 on it.) 'Are you ready for the orange sùm? Put your hand over it so other people can't see it. Don't worry – it's only a bit of fun.'

'Cover it up.'

(Goes through numbers – tells people not to shout out.)

The next one's even easier. 'This is too easy – write in the lemon shape: 5 + 1. (Children call out: 6) No, no, don't shout out.'

(One child has written the answer on the wrong side. Gives another sheet. Continues to hold up cards with sum on, read it out and explain which shape to write in. In between, he tells funny stories about each fruit.):

'Next to the strawberry: answer 4 + 3. Next the pineapple (talks about where pineapple comes from). This is a special sum: 6 + 2. (All cards with sums on also have dots on.) (Tells stories about plums and elephants in Africa – elephants got drunk on plums.) In the plum shape: 5 + 4. You should have one shape left at the bottom, a peach shape. Here comes an easy sum: 1 + 6.'

(Playtime bell has gone)

(Asks one child on each table to collect papers)

'I think I made that too easy. I'm going to have to give out lots of housepoints. If you like that puzzle, shall we try that again on Monday with some harder sums?'

Children: 'Yes, Yes.' (All enjoyed it.)

While the teacher has successfully presented MA 3 as a game/competition which the children appear to have enjoyed, the other Year 2 teacher has taken a different approach. She carried out the SAT in a straightforward way, more like a 'mental arithmetic' test. She commented that the children tightened up a lot, sat back in their seats, drawing in their breath, and appeared rather stressed. 'It was so unlike the way we normally work', she commented.

(Fieldnotes, St. Anne's School)

This lack of standardization in the presentation of SATs, even within one school is not unusual.

The effect of pupil anxiety

In other cases, however, it was not possible for teachers either to allay children's anxiety or to reduce the awareness of a testing situation. In some cases, this was because the children were already anxious and aware of what was involved before the testing situation.

Gemma finishes and gives her sheet to the teacher. Afterwards the teacher asks Gemma the 3 subtraction sums she had wrong. Gemma instantly answers perfectly. The teacher discusses this: Should she consider that Gemma knows the work or not? She wonders whether the SAT is chiefly designed to test children's ability to do the calculations involved or their ability to apply their knowledge in the context of using money. Sharon is extremely conscientious in scrupulously keeping to time allowances for 'quick recall' activities and in cases like Gemma's, when she tries to examine the aims behind the task: very different from the situation at Meadway, where the teacher was cheerfully open about 'bending the rules'.

(Fieldnotes, Leigh School)

Anxiety was particularly marked in some maths SATs involving mental arithmetic where children were under pressure to get the right answer in a given time.

Differences between teachers in the amount of help given

As well as the lack of standardization caused by variations in the amount of help that a teacher felt required to give to different children in the class, there was also considerable variability *between* teachers themselves in this respect.

An important source of possible variation in SAT outcomes centres on different practices of teachers in interpreting the performance of children. Despite the strict instructions surrounding the Maths 3 1992 test, for example, in which the context for testing and the criteria of performance were unambiguously defined, the research team observed many variations in the way in which teachers actually introduced and judged the SATs. Some were very flexible in the timing allowed for doing the sums; others allowed children more than one attempt at the task; or provided aids in the form of flashcards; or other kinds of help to facilitate children answering.

In some cases, the teacher may have given less help than she was allowed to.

The teacher and I look through the Maths sheets. The teacher seems quite upset as she looks at each one. She names children who can do it but they've got muddled up or something.

Some have not concentrated: 'Oh dear, I think they can get one wrong but I'll have to check. It means I won't have many Level 2s. They'll all be Level 1s. I think I may have done it wrong.'

The teacher checks the Teacher's Book for procedures and discovers that she should have helped the children to write in the first example on Sheet 3. This is the one where the children have to give change, that has caught out most children.

'Oh dear, I've made a mistake.'

We go into the staffroom for coffee, the teacher clutching the Teacher's Book to check for further details. She decides that she will ask individual children to think about their answers to Maths 3 in the afternoon 'to see if the penny drops'.

'Well, they can do it, I know, but they haven't done it and I should have helped them more so we'll see if they can do it.'

There is a lot of sympathy. Teacher: 'What is it all for?'

Other teachers: 'It's for the parents. It doesn't help us at all.'

The teacher is not trying to cheat. She simply wants the test to reflect validly what she feels the children can do, to the extent that it does not, then she is prepared to manipulate it.

Later. The teacher has spent the afternoon checking children who 'had not understood what to do in the morning'. She judged that 6 had been able to pass Level 2 'in fact because they had succeeded when the example was explained'.

(Fieldnotes, St. Bede's)

Our fieldnotes record many examples of teachers giving differential degrees of help to different children and groups or interpreting performance in ways more or less different from the regulations because they feel that the child in question is truly worthy of a particular level.

Other examples of more overt departure from the SAT instructions include, for example in the 1992 Maths 3, Sheet 1, children looking at each other's answers and copying; in Maths 3, Sheet 2, children shouting out the answers; or in other schools allowing children to count on their fingers even though this is explicitly not allowed.

Chantelle is doing the change exercise for Maths 3.

Chantelle: 'What must I do now?'

Teacher: 'You take 15p to the shop, put out 15p, now take away your 12p.'

Chantelle does so and enters the right answer. She does the next sum correctly with no help. Chantelle reads: '8p + 6p.'

She counts 13p, writes this, puts out 20p, enters 7p as change from 20p. She quickly does the last sum correctly. Jason asks the teacher for help with the first sum. The teacher goes through the steps with him. He arrives at the right answer. The next sum, 12p + 7p, he puts out the coins and writes 1p. He looks at the coins, takes the sheet to the teacher: 'Miss, what do I do next?'

Teacher: 'What do they cost?'

Jason: '19p.'

Teacher (pointing to '20p'): 'How much do you take to the shop?'

Jason: '20p.'

Teacher: 'So, put out the coins and find out how much you have left.'

Jason returns, puts out 20p, takes out 19p, enters '1'. He goes through the addition 8p + 6p of the next sum correctly and enters 14p. He correctly puts out 20p, takes 14p out, stares at the 14p.

Jason: 'Miss, 14p, take away 20p . . .'

Teacher: 'No, not 14 . . . 20. You need 20p to start with.'

Jason: 'I haven't got enough.' (He has, in fact.)

Teacher: 'Get some more, then.'

Jason silently moves the coins around, writes '5' in the box (for 20p − 14p). For the last sum, he writes '15' (for 6p + 7p).

Teacher: 'Will you check that, Jason. Put them out again.'

Jason: 'Will you help me?'

Teacher: 'I am helping you. Put out 6 and 7.'

Jason does so. Jason: 'It's 13p.'

Teacher: 'Change your answer to 13, then.'

Jason: 'It *is* 13.'

Teacher: 'No, you've written 15.'

She alters 13 to 15. Jason waits for further help.

Teacher: 'Now put out 15p and take 13p away.'

Jason writes 2p in the box. He takes it to the teacher. 4 of the 5 sums are marked right.

(Chantelle finished in 6 minutes, with very little help. Jason needed help at every step, and took 20 minutes.) The teacher has to deal with Angus. He hits Chantelle with a brush; she pushes him. The teacher and (Mary) have to pull him off and hold him away.

The teacher (entering the results in her assessment book): 'I'm in a muddle here – I'm not sure I should record them as reaching this level when I've had to help them so much, but I'm going to, anyway. (All have Level 2.) I'll try some on Level 3, but I don't think they're going to get it. I didn't think she'd manage that.'

(Fieldnotes, Meadway School)

A very different kind of variation was illustrated in another classroom where the children were having a discussion, as part of a science SAT in 1991, about pollution.

Teacher:	'Now, have you seen this?' (Shows big plastic pond liner.)
Teacher:	'Just a minute, boys.' (Teacher draws girls in to speak.)
Teacher:	'Do you think a cat will get into our conservation area?'
Children:	'No, as the cats can't get in.'
Teacher:	'That's right, so it's a safe place for fish and birds. Yes, how do they come in?'
Kevin:	'They fly.'
Teacher:	'Yes, so why is it a safe place?'
Child:	'Because the cats can't get in.'
Teacher:	'Yes, so we've got birds coming in and now we're making something more special with our pond. So what do birds like when you have a pond?'
Child:	'Slugs.'
Teacher:	'Well, so what do all animals like? What do we all need?'
Child:	'Water.'
Teacher:	'Good, because we can't manage without water. It will be special for . . .'
Child:	'Fish.'
Teacher:	'And the birds, yes.'
Teacher:	'And then we've got to be very careful, haven't we? Any ideas, Maria?'
Maria:	−(Silence)
Teacher:	'Well, OK. Laura?'
Laura:	'Perhaps the fox might come, and dogs could.'

> *Teacher*: 'Well, it wasn't what I was thinking – once our pond is finished, what do we have to do and be careful of?'
>
> Kevin suggests netting to keep the dogs off.
>
> *Teacher*: 'Ok, do you think we need a net for our pond?'
> *Emma*: 'My uncle makes (?) (?) paths.'
> *Teacher*: 'We are going to make an area that's nice. And what would we have to do if we saw an infant dropping a crisp packet?'
> *Kevin*: 'Say tidy up.'
> *Teacher*: 'Yes.'
>
> (Fieldnotes, Meadway School)

These fieldnotes illustrate the situation in which the teacher is seeking the right answer from the children as defined by her in relation to a constantly shifting agenda. The teacher is careful to draw the girls into the discussion and to control the dominance of Kevin but she dominates the discussion herself and the children have to guess her mind. This kind of interpersonal domination by the teacher which may facilitate or discourage the oral performance of children is explored in more detail in Filer (1993) but clearly will have an effect on how capable, orally, the teacher defines the children to be. In relation to the above excerpt the teacher herself said later:

> I found I was chasing them round the houses today to get them to say things.

Overview

In sum then, we can say that in both years studied there were enormous variations in the manageability, conduct and interpretation of SATs. Variation was caused both by differences in the opportunities provided for children to perform at their best and by the interpretation of that performance by the teachers. The data suggest that SATs conducted with a keen, able group of children, enjoying the teacher's undivided attention, where the teacher herself is confident and still interested in the task, will elicit the children's best performance, avoid most of the anxiety, and provide for reasonable standardization. At the other extreme, where the task itself may involve considerable creativity and thus interpretation in the marking, or collaboration between children, or where it is too difficult for some children or where the teacher has little or no help in the classroom so that she can work with the SAT group, the children are likely to perform well below their optimum level, their performance variously affected by anxiety, distractions, interference from other children, and copying from each other.

The data suggest that teachers who are already working in the more difficult circumstances of larger numbers of more disruptive children, where there are less resources for additional support, are the very teachers who need to guide and intervene more to elicit children's optimum performance. Such teachers are likely to be those who have to intervene more to help children through the task and are likely to be more troubled about the position of levels. The fact that even the highly standardized SATs were subject to very considerable variation, both in the management of the task and in the circumstances in which the children were able to work, suggests that what many would see as the obvious answer of providing more short, sharp tests, may not in fact be the solution to providing greater standardization.

While such tests may superficially appear to meet the perceived need for objective information about children's levels of achievement, they will in practice still embody an enormous amount of variation in the *context* for performance and will in addition have very limited utility. Indeed, they are likely to be quite counter-productive in terms of at least two of the four purposes of national assessment, the diagnostic and the formative. While written tests would appear to offer relative ease of administration and greater comparability between schools, they are also likely to produce extremely limited information. They may also result in teaching to the test and constrain the National Curriculum in ways which would be unacceptable.

In this respect it is interesting to contrast teachers' views of the teacher assessment (TA) component of SATs which was felt to have caused little or no disruption to normal classroom routine, and was felt to be both reasonably accurate and manageable in terms of time. At the same time, these assessments have led to some new insights concerning children's learning for many teachers. Given that all the teachers felt there was a very fair match between the SAT results and TA results, the question must arise of the value of an additional layer of testing which in practice is so unreliable. These points are taken up in more detail in later chapters.

The original blueprint for national assessment, which was set out in the TGAT (1988) Report, identified four different purposes for national assessment: diagnostic assessment to identify individual pupils' strengths and weaknesses; formative assessment to give feedback and encouragement; summative assessment to report on a given pupil's attainment at a given stage of schooling; and evaluative assessment to provide aggregated information about the overall level of pupil achievement in any particular school, as a basis for comparing one school with another. It is immediately clear that SATs do not provide very well for any of these purposes. They are not frequent enough, nor sufficiently integrated into the normal routines and curricular emphases of a given classroom to provide guidance for pupils and teachers about appropriate individual learning targets. Nor are they reliable or detailed enough to provide summative and evaluative information that can be confidently trusted by teachers, parents and the public. Since the SATs come only at the end of a Key Stage and since they identify only very broad levels of attainment, this suggests that the latter is their real purpose. Our data suggest that in the context of primary education in England and Wales in which the ideology of child-centred education is still central, it is not possible to devise any assessment task or test to be implemented by teachers which will not be subject to very considerable contextual effects. One might wish to go further and argue that any attempt to test 7-year-olds on a systematic basis is bound to be heavily overlaid in its results by contextual effects, including who does the teaching, in what circumstances, and what is the personal affective state of the child concerned. Even if such tests were superficially reliable – for example, if they were multiple choice, like those which are used widely in Japan and the USA – their validity would be very questionable.

Yet the many strongly worded criticisms of SATs, which were voiced by teachers, have been almost exclusively concerned with their mode of implementation and use and not with the tasks themselves. Rather, these have been generally appreciated. So has the increased liaison between colleagues, the increased contact with parents and the provision of moderation arrangements which teachers see as the result of a more formal obligation to engage in teacher assessment.

The way forward

It is apparent that there is now an international trend towards more broadly based performance assessment which is conducted by teachers. It would appear that much educational benefit can be derived where teachers are challenged to be more professional in their assessment practice and are provided with materials to support them in their task of identifying the complex web of strengths and needs that characterize the individual learner. But while the policy priorities behind the development of performance assessment initiatives typically include this agenda, they equally tend also to embrace the very different agenda of institutional and system accountability. In this kind of 'high stakes' context, evidence such as that included in this chapter, which suggests that performance assessment cannot be detached in practice from the mediatory effects of teachers' professional strategies and judgement, must give rise for concern. Given the choice between narrow, but relatively reliable, 'high stakes' assessment and valid, but relatively unreliable, 'high stakes' assessment, the only tenable strategy would appear to be to abandon attempts to make aggregated judgements of institutional or system-wide standards on the basis of 'high stakes' assessments. Rather what is needed is a different combination of approaches. For standards monitoring this should involve a light-sample-based and hence 'low stakes' performance assessment approach like that pioneered in England by the APU. Such an approach could be combined with the use of carefully structured, and externally supported, performance assessments backed up by a portfolio of evidence both to facilitate the process of teaching and learning and to improve communication with parents and other users. By contrast, as long as assessment data are used as the basis for league tables and the like, the potential of performance assessment to enhance learning is unlikely to be realized and grave injustices may be done to many schools and children.

Acknowledgement

This chapter is based on the work of an ESRC research project (grant reference number R000234673) involving Dorothy Abbott, Andrew Pollard, Marilyn Osborn and Paul Croll. More details of the research project reported here are included in Pollard *et al.* (1994) *Changing English Primary Schools*, London, Cassell (1994).

Appendix 1.1 Defining 'benchmarks' (Western Australia)

MATERIALS DEVELOPED FOR THE PROGRAM

The **benchmarks, What to look for statements** and **assessment tasks** were developed from selected phases/stages of the English and mathematics syllabuses. Because they are linked directly to the respective syllabus documents, the benchmarks reflect the content and methodologies of each subject. They were developed in collaboration with practising teachers and were subject to scrutiny by other educators and community representatives.

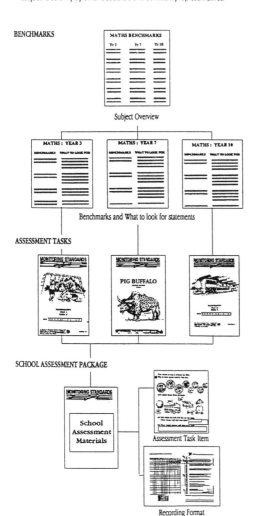

BENCHMARKS

Subject Overview

Benchmarks and What to look for statements

ASSESSMENT TASKS

SCHOOL ASSESSMENT PACKAGE

Assessment Task Item

Recording Format

BENCHMARKS

The **benchmarks** have been written in behavioural terms to enable observations and judgements to be made about student performance.

WHAT TO LOOK FOR STATEMENTS

What to look for statements provide examples of what to look for when making judgements as to whether or not a student is working at the benchmark.

ASSESSMENT TASKS

Assessment tasks were developed to monitor performance in relation to the benchmarks. They are not intended as 'minimum competency' tests but focus on the range of skills evident within each year level. The tasks have been developed around a theme or within a context which is consistent with the syllabus. This allows the students to write about and solve problems within situations that are meaningful to them. The assessment tasks were administered to a sample of students in Years 3, 7 and 10.

ASSESSMENT MATERIALS

Assessment materials for English and mathematics will be made available for schools during Term 2, 1991. The package will include assessment tasks, marking guides, record sheets and reporting guidelines. These will allow teachers and schools to monitor the performance of their students and to compare this performance to system-wide results.

Appendix 1.2   Defining 'benchmarks' (Western Australia)

BENCHMARK	WHAT TO LOOK FOR
7	
LEVEL OF UNDERSTANDING Using appropriate texts, the student is able to locate significant information (both implicit and explicit), recall details in a sequential order, summarise the relevant information, recognise relationships between ideas and substantiate personal evaluations.	There is evidence that the student can: • identify the form, e.g., *report, description, graph, myth, interview*; • accurately locate and recall relevant information from print and non-print forms - in a sequential order when appropriate; • infer information from print and non-print forms, i.e., cause / effect and problem / solution relationships; emotion from clues located throughout the text; • infer the meaning of figurative language, e.g., *as light as a feather*; • categorise and classify information; • recognise the underlying concepts of words, e.g., *'magpie' as distinct from the less precise 'bird' may imply a large black and white bird that swoops people'*; • identify ambiguous and inconsistent messages in print and non-print forms; • connect and synthesise two ideas separated within a text or between texts; • make simple evaluations and judgements about the text; • substantiate answers to questions using text information and background knowledge where appropriate.
3	
LEVEL OF UNDERSTANDING Using appropriate written and graphic texts the student recalls explicit information and infers implicit information. Unsubstantiated judgements may be made.	There is evidence that the student can: • obtain meaning from simple tables and diagrams; • demonstrate understanding by drawing to complement the text; • recognise cause and effect relationships, e.g., *'We can't go to the zoo today because it is raining.'*; • retell a few significant events in sequential order; • identify explicit information, e.g., *characters, time and place*; • identify the emotions of characters, e.g., *the man was sad*; • construct meaning from simple figurative language, e.g., *he was as white as a sheet means that he looked pale and unwell or scared*; • elaborate answers to questions, e.g., *it is a scary story because it's about a mean old witch who eats children*; • follow simple written directions.

Appendix 1.3   Defining 'benchmarks' (Ontario, Canada)

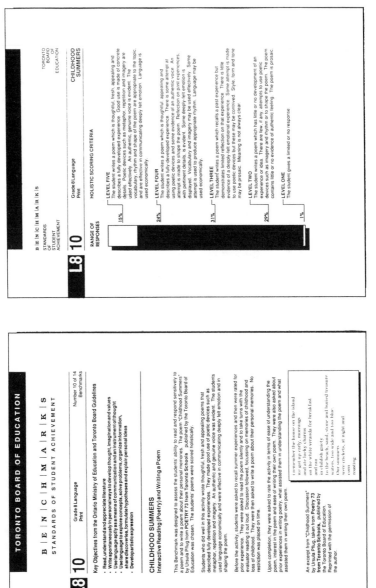

Key Objectives from the Ontario Ministry of Education and Toronto Board Guidelines
- Read, understand and appreciate literature
- Write spontaneously in personal ways to develop thought, imagination and values
- Use language aptly as a means of communication and an instrument of thought
- Use language to explore concepts, solve problems, organize information, share discoveries, formulate hypotheses and explain personal ideas
- Develop artistic expression

CHILDHOOD SUMMERS
Interactive Reading (Poetry) and Writing a Poem

This Benchmark was designed to assess the students' ability to read and respond sensitively to a poem and to write a poem about their personal memories. The poem "Childhood Summers" by Ursula Plug from POETRY 73 from Toronto Schools, published by the Toronto Board of Education was chosen. The students' poems were scored holistically.

Students who did well in this activity wrote thoughtful, fresh and appealing poems that described fully developed experiences. They made good use of poetic devices such as metaphor, repetition and imagery. An authentic and genuine voice was evident. The students used language economically and were effective in communicating deeply felt emotion and in shaping the poem.

Before the activity, students were asked to recall summer experiences and then were rated for prior experience. They were asked to read the poem silently and to take turns with the evaluator reading it out loud. Discussion followed, focussing on memories of childhood and loss of childhood. The students were then asked to write a poem about their personal memories. No restriction was placed on time.

Upon completion, they were asked to rate the activity in terms of ease of understanding the poem, interest in the poem and ease of writing their own poem. They were also asked about prior experiences in writing poetry, what assisted them in understanding the poem and what assisted them in writing their own poem.

An excerpt from "Childhood Summers" by Ursula Plug, taken from Poetry 73 from Toronto Schools, published by the Toronto Board of Education. Reprinted with the permission of the author.

> I remember the house on the island
> we got up early, mornings
> and ate lucky charms
> on the white veranda for breakfast
> and ran
> in childish glee
> to the beach, sand, stone and buried treasure
> waters, two wide and too blue
> Our summers
> were crickets, at night and
> corn
> roasting

HOLISTIC SCORING CRITERIA

LEVEL FIVE
The student writes a poem which is thoughtful, fresh, appealing and describes a fully developed experience. Good use is made of concrete details. Poetic devices such as metaphor, repetition and imagery are used effectively. An authentic, genuine voice is evident. The vocabulary, rhythm and shape of the poem are appropriate to the topic, and are effective in communicating deeply felt emotion. Language is used economically.
15%

LEVEL FOUR
The student writes a poem which is thoughtful, appealing and describes a fully developed experience. There is some attempt at using poetic devices and some evidence of an authentic voice. An attempt is made to shape the poem. Reflection on past experiences with pertinent details is evident. Some deeply felt emotion is displayed. Vocabulary and imagery may be used effectively. Some attempt is used to produce appropriate rhythm. Language may be used economically.
24%

LEVEL THREE
The student writes a poem which recalls a past experience but demonstrates limited reflection on that experience. There is little evidence of a deeply felt emotional experience. Some attempt is made to use poetic devices but these may be contrived. Style, form and tone may be prosaic. Meaning is not always clear.
31%

LEVEL TWO
The student writes a poem which has little or no development of an experience or idea. There are few, if any, attempts to use poetic devices such as imagery and rhythm or to shape the poem. The poem contains little or no evidence of authentic feeling. The poem is prosaic.
20%

LEVEL ONE
The student gives a limited or no response.
1%

RANGE OF RESPONSES

Appendix 1.4 Standard assessment tasks for 7-year-olds (England and Wales)

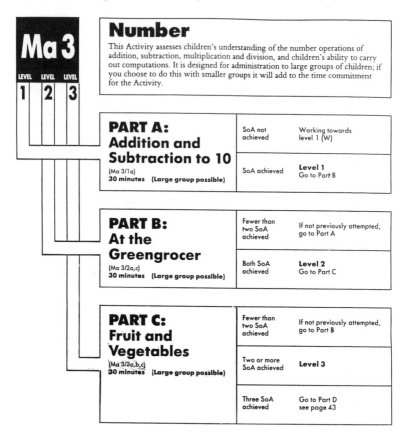

Ma 3

LEVEL LEVEL LEVEL

1 **2** **3**

Number

This Activity assesses children's understanding of the number operations of addition, subtraction, multiplication and division, and children's ability to carry out computations. It is designed for administration to large groups of children; if you choose to do this with smaller groups it will add to the time commitment for the Activity.

| **PART A:** **Addition and Subtraction to 10** (Ma 3/1a) **30 minutes (Large group possible)** | SoA not achieved | Working towards level 1 (W) |
| | SoA achieved | **Level 1** Go to Part B |

| **PART B:** **At the Greengrocer** (Ma 3/2a,c) **30 minutes (Large group possible)** | Fewer than two SoA achieved | If not previously attempted, go to Part A |
| | Both SoA achieved | **Level 2** Go to Part C |

PART C: **Fruit and Vegetables** (Ma 3/3a,b,c) **30 minutes (Large group possible)**	Fewer than two SoA achieved	If not previously attempted, go to Part B
	Two or more SoA achieved	**Level 3**
	Three SoA achieved	Go to Part D see page 43

Ma 3

LEVEL **1**   LEVEL **2**   LEVEL **3**

PART A:
Addition and Subtraction
to 10

Resources

Each child will need a copy of Ma 3 *Pupil Sheet 1*, a pen or pencil, and ten counters, of the kind you normally use.

What to do
Large-group procedure

◆ Help the children to work out the first addition and the first subtraction on Ma 3 *Pupil Sheet 1*, as an introduction.

This is not assessed. Although the additions and subtractions are listed on the same sheet, there is no need for the children to do them all at the same time, or in the order listed.

◆ Ask each child to complete Ma 3 *Pupil Sheet 1*, using counters to work out the answers.

You may give the children any help they need in reading the *Pupil Sheet*, but they must work out the computations without help in order to demonstrate evidence of attainment.

◆ If you are working with a small group, ask each child to perform the computations on Ma 3 *Pupil Sheet 1*.

You may do this orally, or using the *Pupil Sheet*, or rewriting the *Pupil Sheet* in a form with which the children are familiar (for example, 2 and 3 instead of 2 + 3). However you decide to approach it, each child should carry out the same 10 computations without help (after the initial examples) in order to demonstrate evidence of attainment.

LEVEL 2   LEVEL 3

PART B:
At the Greengrocer

Resources

Each child will need a copy of Ma 3 *Pupil Sheets 2* and *3* and a pen or pencil. For *Pupil Sheet 3* children may use money or play money or counters if this is your normal practice.

If you decide to work with a small group, you may wish to use real or play fruits marked with the prices.

What to do
Large-group procedure

◆ Give each of the children a copy of Ma 3 *Pupil Sheet 2*.

◆ Explain that you are going to read out some additions and subtractions very quickly, and that they should write each answer in the fruit you name.

In explaining the work, use whatever words you and the children are used to. The fruits are a way of showing children where to write their answers without the possible confusion that might be caused by numbering.

◆ Ask the children to look at the blue column of fruits. Read out '2 + 1'; explain that they should write the answer '3' in the apple. Tell them that the following ones will need to be done very quickly. Explain that they should work down the page filling in the answers in the fruits.

◆ Then read out the following additions, allowing children *no more than 5 seconds to answer each one*:

    4 + 4 (orange)
    1 + 5 (lemon)
    3 + 7 (pear)
    4 + 3 (strawberry)
    6 + 2 (pineapple)
    5 + 4 (plum)
    1 + 6 (peach)

For example, say 'Four plus four; write the answer in the orange', and so on.

This assessment is aimed at children's ability to recall number facts without calculating, so it is important to allow them no more than 5 seconds to answer. Reassure children by telling them that they can leave a blank and move on to the next one if unable to answer quickly. Some children respond well if this is presented as a game or race; in any case, present it in a relaxed way so that children do not become worried if unable to keep up.

Part B continues

LEVEL 2 LEVEL 3

Large-group procedure *(continued)*

You may write the additions and subtractions on flash cards or a chalk board if you wish, but children must not be able to see any one for more than 5 seconds.

◆ Then tell the children to look at the red column of fruits.

◆ Read out '3 – 1'; explain that they should write the answer '2' in the apple. Tell them that the following ones will need to be done very quickly. Explain that they should work down the page, filling in the answers in the fruits.

◆ Then read out the following subtractions, allowing children *no more than 5 seconds to answer each one*:

For example, say 'Nine minus four; write the answer in the orange', and so on.

> 9 – 4 (orange)
> 7 – 5 (lemon)
> 4 – 3 (pear)
> 10 – 7 (strawberry)
> 9 – 6 (pineapple)
> 8 – 2 (plum)
> 5 – 3 (peach)

◆ Give each of the children a copy of Ma 3 *Pupil Sheet 3*. Help them to work out the first addition and subtraction and to write the answers in the boxes.

◆ There is not a time limit for this *Pupil Sheet*.

◆ Ask them to complete the rest of the sheet by themselves. They may use counters or money if this is your normal practice.

You may give any help necessary in reading the words on the sheet, but children must perform the calculations without help to demonstrate evidence of attainment.

◆ If you are working with a small group, ask each child all of the eight additions and eight subtractions given above. The first addition and the first subtraction should be discussed as an example and not assessed.

You may do this in oral or written form, and vary the order of the questions, but each of the children should do the same 16 questions that appear above.

Part B continues

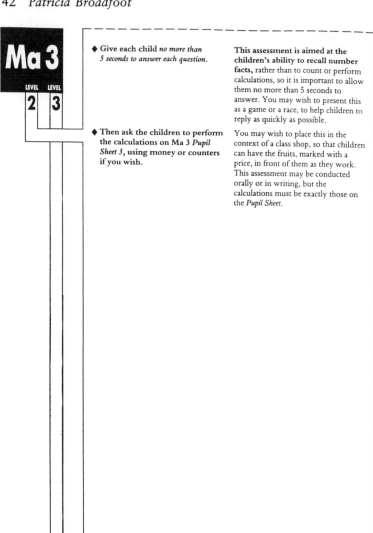

Ma 3

LEVEL **2**   LEVEL **3**

♦ Give each child *no more than 5 seconds to answer each question.*

This assessment is aimed at the children's ability to recall number facts, rather than to count or perform calculations, so it is important to allow them no more than 5 seconds to answer. You may wish to present this as a game or a race, to help children to reply as quickly as possible.

♦ Then ask the children to perform the calculations on Ma 3 *Pupil Sheet 3*, using money or counters if you wish.

You may wish to place this in the context of a class shop, so that children can have the fruits, marked with a price, in front of them as they work. This assessment may be conducted orally or in writing, but the calculations must be exactly those on the *Pupil Sheet*.

One box has 6 apples.

How many apples are there in 4 boxes?

One bag has 8 oranges.

How many oranges in 6 bags?

One crate holds 10 pineapples.

How many crates are needed for 70 pineapples?

2

TEACHER INVOLVEMENT IN NEW APPROACHES TO ASSESSMENT

Harry Torrance

Authentic assessment and the improvement of teaching

Many claims have been made in recent years about the potentially positive effects of new forms of assessment on the quality of the teaching and learning process and the standard of outcomes produced by the process. As discussed in the Introduction to this volume, such claims derive from a variety of arguments which relate to issues of curriculum quality and curriculum development, and to questions of how children learn. In particular, it is argued that the quality of teaching will be improved, with respect to both curriculum coverage and teaching methods, if higher-order skills and competencies such as problem-solving, investigation and analysis are included in what is to be assessed (see, for example, ILEA 1984; Murphy and Torrance 1988; Gifford and O'Connor 1992; Office of Technology Assessment (OTA) 1992).

However, it is not at all clear exactly how the process of improvement might be brought about and in this respect debates about the relationship between assessment, curriculum quality and learning have begun to overlap with more overtly political debates about standards, accountability and the possibility of leading changes in schooling by instigating changes in assessment. In the UK changes implemented in this context have been referred to as assessment-led curriculum development (Gipps 1986; Horton 1987; Grant 1989), in the USA as measurement-driven instruction (MDI) (Popham 1987). Thus assessment is being identified as a key mechanism for monitoring and intervening in the educational process, with attention being paid to the role of assessment in the education system *as a system* (as distinct from its implications for individual life chances), and with key research questions being framed less in terms of the extent to which assessments measure what they purport to measure (important though this still is) and more in terms of what impact assessment might have on the instructional process.

Originally the debate over MDI seemed to overlap with criticisms of narrow approaches to testing *per se* (Bracey 1987), but more recently it has moved on as the possibilities of developing more authentic approaches to assessment have been explored. Of course, there is no necessary connection between MDI and authentic assessment and indeed some may well see them as antithetical. Certainly one can envisage developments in new forms of assessment progressing in tandem with changes in the curriculum and teaching methods (releasing instruction, as it were, from the straightjacket of paper-and-pencil testing) without also arguing that such new forms of assessment should *drive* teaching and learning. Yet such connections have been made so that, as Nickerson (1989: 6) put it:

> a truly adequate approach to educational assessment . . . not only will measure accurately what has been learned but will also provide useful diagnostic information for future instruction and . . . will help drive the system as a whole, toward increasing effectiveness in the nurturing of understanding and thinking.

Likewise the recent report by the OTA (1992: 11) stated:

> advocates of new ways to test often argue that since tests can play a powerful role in influencing learning, they must be designed to support desired educational goals. These advocates disparage 'teaching to the test' when a test calls for

isolated facts from a multiple-choice format, but endorse the concept when the test consists of 'authentic' tasks.

However, these expanded visions of the problem of validity, and optimistic views about the potentially positive impact of assessment on teaching and learning, seem to take a very mechanistic view of the implementation process: improve the test and you will improve the teaching. But just because poor assessment practices can impact negatively on teaching and learning, it does not automatically follow that better assessment practices will impact positively. In fact, as Cohen and Spillane (1992: 19) note, at least with respect to the United States, 'little is known about the operation of innovative assessments, let alone their effects'. In particular, the role of the classroom teacher in possibly inhibiting change (Airasian 1988) and certainly being crucial to its mediation and ultimate success (Stake 1991a) has received relatively little attention.

Problems of implementation

In reviewing the conditions under which measurement might have most impact on instruction (in particular, the combining of high stakes with high standards) Airasian (1988) also explores the role which authentic assessment might play in our definition of high standards. In so doing, he draws attention to both the theoretical problem of adequately conceptualizing and articulating how it is that higher-order skills and understandings can be taught, and the practical problem of whether or not teachers are willing and able to implement new subject matter and teaching methods.

There is also the question of teacher involvement in the assessment process itself. By definition, authentic approaches to assessment will engage students in more complex tasks than hitherto – extended assignments which might involve the investigation of a problem and the production of essays or reports, charts, diagrams, practical artefacts and so on. Some of these tasks and products could be set and marked by agencies outside the school, but this would leave them at a level of artificiality which would deny the more ambitious claims for authentic assessment; in particular, leaving unassessed the ephemeral *processes* of investigating, analysing and problem-solving which proponents of authentic assessment would claim to be of equal if not greater importance than its products. So teachers are likely to be drawn into the formal assessment of students' work in the classroom in a way in which they have not been before.

Certainly this has been the case in the United Kingdom and it has raised a number of issues with respect to teachers' perceptions of what it is they think they are becoming involved in (a new approach to assessment, or teaching, or both) and whether the benefits which have derived from small-scale voluntaristic involvement in development programmes can be readily generalized to large-scale non-voluntaristic national implementation. Evidence from a number of different initiatives in the UK over the last ten years or so consistently points to the need for teachers to understand the curricular and pedagogic implications of their becoming involved in new approaches to assessment in order that the benefits of their involvement can be maximized.

Interpreting and mediating new approaches to assessment

Thus, for example, the 'national criteria' of the General Certificate of Secondary Education (GCSE),[1] which was introduced in England and Wales in 1986, specified that significant elements of teacher-assessed coursework and practical work should be written into new syllabuses submitted for inclusion in the overall system. Prior to this teachers could choose from a variety of GCE and CSE syllabuses and modes of examination and decide for themselves whether or not they wished to be involved in coursework and/or practical assessment (usually known as school-based assessment – see the Introduction to this volume). Many did choose to be involved, but many more did not; the majority stuck with the traditional and straightforward end-of-course written examination.

Of those who did choose to become involved in more varied and demanding approaches to assessment, the reasons for involvement varied considerably but essentially reflected a desire either to introduce a new approach to teaching their subject, or to assess it more flexibly. Thus, for example, some wished to introduce more practical work into science, or more local studies including fieldwork into history, geography and social studies, and this in turn brought with it the necessity of assessing such work *in situ*; others wished to provide shorter-term goals and an incremental (continuous) approach to assessment and grading for students whom they perceived to be disadvantaged by end-of-course one-off final examinations (Torrance 1982; 1984; 1986a[2]). Sometimes these two motives were combined, but the important point to note is that it was involvement in curriculum decision-making and development which seemed to be the more positive motive and bring about the most effective involvement in the assessment process. Teachers had to *want* to integrate teaching and assessment in order to make the most of the opportunities for more flexible teaching which more flexible approaches to assessment offered.

Evidence from less formal examples of teacher involvement in school-based assessment confirms the importance of parallel involvement in curriculum development as a primary source of motivation and professional support. One such example is that of 'graded tests' whereby groups of teachers produced short modular schemes of work for students on a local basis, accompanied by regular end-of-module or end-of-unit tests, graded in terms of syllabus content and level of difficulty (ILEA 1984; Pennycuick and Murphy 1988). The intention behind such schemes seemed once again to be to introduce more relevant, practical and meaningful content into the secondary school curriculum, and to provide students with shorter-term learning goals, feedback on progress and, sometimes, an incremental 'ladder' towards final examination success (in such cases the graded test scheme would be linked to an examining board syllabus). The initial interest and development work stemmed from teachers themselves, however, or teachers working in collaboration with local university subject experts and/or local education authority advisers. Thus 'teacher enthusiasm for schemes is based at least as much on the prospect of achieving desired curricular and pedagogical reform as on graded test principles' (Pennycuick 1988: 72). Whether enthusiasm and quality can be sustained in the long term, when the innovation becomes the norm, or when involvement is national and compulsory is another matter.

Certainly with regard to formal involvement in school-based assessment, where involvement was not voluntary – for example, where an examination board introduced coursework into its syllabuses for the first time, or perhaps where a new head of department insisted on all his or her staff changing to a new syllabus involving school-based assessment – considerable confusion was often created as to why this was happening and considerable resentment expressed at the extra workload involved (additional marking, record-keeping, and so on). In particular, if the change was thought to be purely for the purpose of improving the validity and reliability of the assessment (a not unreasonable assumption for teachers to make if the change was initiated by the examination board), then problems of implementation were interpreted in these traditional assessment terms with queries and anxieties being expressed about the subjectivity of teacher marking, the criteria to be used, how grades would be made comparable across schools, and so on. Discussions of how the change might broaden the curriculum and improve the process of *teaching* did not figure very largely in these circumstances – that issue had to be on the agenda already: simply becoming involved in the assessment process did not automatically stimulate such discussion (Torrance 1986a).

These problems were repeated on a much larger scale when GCSE was introduced and all secondary school teachers involved with examination classes had to engage to some degree in school-based assessment (the weighting of coursework varied from 20% to 100%, depending on the subject and syllabus followed). The new examining system was in fact launched with the general intention of promoting 'improvements in the secondary school curriculum and the ways in which subjects are taught' (Department of Education and Science (DES) 1985a) and syllabuses were reviewed to accord with centrally produced 'national criteria'. However, the inclusion of elements of school-based assessment was argued for specifically in terms of improving the validity and reliability of the assessment process:

Internally-assessed components may serve one or more of the following purposes . . .
a) to assess objectives which cannot be assessed externally;
b) to assess objectives different from those for a written [i.e. externally examined] component;
c) to provide a complementary assessment of the same objectives as a written component;

   d) to assess objectives for which there is only ephemeral
   evidence.

                                                    (DES 1985b: 5–6)

The examining boards were charged with the formal responsibility
of organizing the subsequent programme of induction and in-
service training, and not surprisingly the main topics of concern
were the criteria and procedures for assessment – the minutia of
marking, record-keeping and reporting – rather than 'improvements in the secondary school curriculum' (Radnor 1987; Grant
1989).[3]
   This is not to say that more general discussions about changes
in curriculum and teaching methods did not take place at all, but
rather to note that they took place at the level of the individual
school or subject department, and over a much longer period of
time than any simple notion of 'implementation' might imply, as
teachers gained experience of the new approach and adapted their
work accordingly. An evaluation of the introduction of GCSE
carried out at the National Foundation for Educational Research
(NFER) identified three broad categories of teacher response: 'the
committed innovator', 'the willing recruit' and 'the reluctant con-
script' (Grant 1989: 97). These categories seemed, at least in part,
to reflect teachers' previous experience (or lack of it) with school-
based assessment. There are also many echoes in Grant's account
of more general problems to do with the promotion and management of change (cf. Fullan 1991, for a general review of such
issues; and also Ball and Bowe 1992, with specific regard to the
new National Curriculum). However, these problems were compounded by the particular tensions and pressures engendered by the
innovation in question being concerned with assessment and being
perceived by teachers first and foremost in these terms – to do
with accuracy and fairness with respect to students' future life
chances, allied to questions of school accountability – rather than
wider concerns with curriculum improvement. The imperatives of
examining framed the way in which the innovation was interpreted
and teachers drew on their previous experience and understandings of what assessment 'is' – their structure of belief about what
constitutes assessment and what its purpose is – in order to make
sense of the changes and make decisions about how they should
implement them. More recent evidence suggests that such an

interpretative framework is still having an effect, with teachers feeling under pressure to produce tasks and assignments which are more 'controlled' than routine classroom work and thus formalizing assessment requirements into special 'coursework lessons' (Peterson 1992). Hewitt (1991) similarly reports special discussions and debates being set up to test 'oral skills' in GCSE English, rather than such skills being assessed more realistically and authentically in the course of ordinary classroom communication.

Another assessment development which has received a great deal of attention in the UK is that of records of achievement. Initially, once again, groups of local teachers became interested in assessing and reporting achievement on more than narrowly academic objectives – how students worked in groups to solve a problem, what sort of initiative and endeavour they manifested, and so on. Portfolios of evidence of achievement began to be collected and profile reports of students' strengths and weaknesses were produced. At the same time ideas began to be developed which placed a dialogue between teacher and student about the student's strengths and weaknesses at the heart of such novel assessment processes (Torrance 1991b). Government funding was then provided for the development of such schemes on a much wider basis. This provided a significant stimulus to grassroots initiatives but also meant that if a local education authority which had successfully bid for funding wanted to develop the initiatives across all schools in its control, many more teachers than the initial enthusiasts were drawn into the process. Obviously there is not space here to review all the ramifications, problems and benefits which ensued. The government-funded evaluation of the records of achievement programme reported increased student motivation and interest in schooling, along with improvements in the process of learning, but also suggested that for such benefits to accrue teachers had to be involved in a lengthy process of induction and development work – they had to understand the broad intentions of the programme and work through many theoretical and practical problems at local level (Broadfoot *et al.* 1988). Other studies have suggested that where funding was provided at a much lower level (for instance, by local education authorities outside the government programme) and where the process of teacher–student dialogue was interpreted too narrowly and treated in too bureaucratic a fashion the intentions of the scheme could be confounded – the process of dialogue became more of a routine chore (for teachers and students alike) than an opportunity for reflection and growth (Pole 1993).

Most recently in the UK, debates about the changing role, purpose and practice of assessment have found concrete expression in the national assessment programme which is being implemented alongside the National Curriculum. The national assessment programme is particularly ambitious in that its intention is to assess all children in all National Curriculum subjects at ages 7, 11, 14 and 16 through a combination of 'teacher assessment' (TA) of coursework (that is, school-based assessment) and teacher administration of externally devised 'Standard Assessment Tasks' (SATs). The overall structure of the system (a National Curriculum with 'Key Stage' testing, the results of which are published) has been devised and introduced within a political agenda concerned largely with accountability and the raising of standards through promoting competition between schools. The specific mechanisms of TA and SATs, along with the content of the tasks themselves, have been devised by groups of educational advisers and consortia of test development agencies working under the auspices of a government-appointed School Examinations and Assessment Council (Task Group on Assessment and Testing (TGAT) 1988; SEAC 1989). The new system is still being developed, is subject to intense political scrutiny, and on occasions direct political interference, but the initial report which set the educational framework for the system attempted to crystallize a good deal of emergent professional opinion concerning the potentially positive benefits of broader approaches to assessment and the role of formative assessment in the promotion of learning:

> Promoting children's learning is a principal aim of schools. Assessment lies at the heart of this process . . . it should be an integral part of the educational process, continually providing both 'feedback' and 'feedforward'. It therefore needs to be incorporated systematically into teaching strategies and practices at all levels
>
> (TGAT 1988: paras 3–4)

This report also recommended that both the TA and SAT elements should involve 'a mixture of . . . tests, practical tasks and observations . . . in order to minimise curriculum distortion' (TGAT 1987:

para. 59). The SEAC (1989: para. 6) went further, suggesting that the new assessment system could lead developments at school level: 'The development agencies will guide training [and] provide opportunities for teachers to learn more about the interpretation of statements of attainment . . . by means of exemplifications'.

These are the arguments which have been used to justify the involvement of teachers in formal assessment procedures across the whole 5–16 age range of compulsory schooling. The TGAT Report in particular promoted the idea of teacher assessment in order to make most use of teachers' close observations of students undertaking a wide variety of tasks. This was in order to maximize the validity of assessments (the issue of authenticity) and provide detailed 'formative feedback' to students. However, the arguments were derived from the sorts of evidence reviewed briefly above – teacher involvement in graded test schemes and records of achievement schemes – two initiatives which were largely grounded in voluntaristic involvement in assessment, the reasons for which were more to do with curriculum and pedagogical development than with improving assessment *per se*. Also both of these initiatives (and GCSE which developed in parallel with them) involved only secondary school teachers – national assessment was to involve teachers at all levels of the system, many of whom, especially at primary level, would have had no previous involvement with formal assessment. Furthermore the whole national assessment programme has been introduced in a political atmosphere which has stressed the role of assessment in measuring achievement, stimulating competition and rendering schools accountable to parents and government. In such circumstances it is these issues, and the traditional notions of assessment which they encompass, which have been most significant in framing teachers interpretations of their new role. Thus, for example, Harlen and Qualter (1991) report that primary school teachers' perceptions of TA involved a clear separation of the processes of teaching and assessment with assessment being interpreted and defined in formal terms. They summarized the differences as follows:

Teaching
Children encouraged to talk to each other
Children not necessarily grouped by 'level'
Children work together, help each other

Nothing written down about performance
Teacher sees how far children can go
Teacher gives help

Assessment
Children work alone
Children warned to 'do their best' and so are aware of being
   assessed
Teacher keeps record of performance
Teacher asks children specific questions
Children grouped by 'level'
Task focussed on Statement of Attainment
                              (Harlen and Qualter 1991: 146)

Similarly, the government's own inspectors of schools report that:

Compared with 1989–90 . . . Some teachers set up activities
specifically so that they could make their assessments; fewer
used their normal classroom activities . . . teachers were
uncertain about how often a child must demonstrate what
was required of a particular Statement [of attainment] . . .
several teachers were planning to use some of the techniques
from the Standard Assessment Tasks in their routine work.
         (Her Majesty's Inspectorate (HMI) 1992: 13, 21)

Thus long-term taken-for-granted notions of what counts as assessment, combined with the political focus on measurement, rather
than instruction, have once again combined, as with the introduction of GCSE, to narrow teachers' understanding of the possibilities
inherent in the new system.

Conclusion

Of course, it must be acknowledged that the intentions and aspirations of 'authentic' assessment and American ideas of 'measurement-
driven instruction' are not the same as UK intentions for and
experience of school-based assessment and teacher assessment. In
particular, it might be argued that the intention of authentic assessment is simply to develop better assessment, which might still be
done quite formally, without striving wholly to integrate teaching
with assessment. Teaching would then be 'driven' in the right

direction, but not directly changed by specific roles and procedures in the assessment process being designated for and assigned to teachers. From this perspective the evidence reported by HMI above would presumably be taken to be quite encouraging – it might be argued that getting teachers to use 'good SATs' is exactly what the designers of authentic assessment would want (see also Chapter 3 in this volume). But this places enormous responsibility on the test designers to 'get it right', and still begs all the issues of interpretation and mediation to which this chapter has been drawing attention. Certainly evidence from the first pilot trial of the new SATs, which involved teachers in administering a series of lengthy authentic tasks to 7-year-olds, suggests that the teachers had enormous difficulty in interpreting, conducting and assessing the tasks – precisely because they were 'authentic', they were too complicated to communicate easily to teachers and too demanding for teachers to conduct under ordinary classroom conditions (Torrance 1993b; see also Chapters 1, 3 and 5 in this volume).

In practice, then, there is likely to be considerable overlap between the UK experience of teacher assessment and US attempts to develop authentic assessment which will drive instruction. While the terms are not synonymous, and the two sets of activities will not be exactly the same, there are probably sufficient similarities for the cautionary UK evidence to be taken seriously. This is not to say that further development of authentic assessment should not be undertaken, on either side of the Atlantic or indeed elsewhere, but rather that it should be undertaken with full regard to problems of teacher interpretation and mediation at school level, and paying considerably more attention to the literature of educational innovation and the management of change than perhaps has generally been the case with respect to changes in assessment practices. The UK evidence is that teachers' capacity and willingness to engage with changes in assessment is particularly influenced by very deep-rooted and long-standing notions of what the purpose of assessment is, and thus they have particular assumptions about what is expected of them when they become involved in it. Teachers have engaged with changes in assessment most enthusiastically and effectively when these changes have derived from, or developed in parallel with, clearly understood changes in the curriculum. But changes in assessment *per se* run the risk of being interpreted within a traditional 'testing paradigm' rather than a 'pedagogical paradigm' and so confounding the best intentions of those developing new forms of assessment. Thus, rather than thinking of authentic assessment 'driving' instruction, it might be more helpful to think of it as providing a new framework for the discussion and development of instruction. However, this intention would have to be made explicit; simply imposing a new form of assessment does not automatically lead to such discussions. New approaches to assessment are certainly a necessary, but not a sufficient mechanism for change within educational systems. Implementation must proceed in tandem with extensive school-based exploration of the problems and possibilities of new approaches to assessment if our ambitions for them are to be realized.

Notes

1 GCSE is a single-subject examination taken by pupils at the end of compulsory schooling (16 years of age). Students will take anything from one or two GCSEs to nine or ten depending on their aptitude and prior achievement.
2 The empirical work referred to was supported by various research grants from the Schools Council and the Southern Region Examinations Board.
3 Such training was in any case very limited: subject heads of department attended a two-day course and were then expected to train staff in school.

3

NATIONAL CURRICULUM ASSESSMENT: EMERGING MODELS OF TEACHER ASSESSMENT IN THE CLASSROOM

Bet McCallum, Caroline Gipps, Shelley McAlister and Margaret Brown

Introduction

The Education Reform Act (ERA) of 1988 brought about wide-ranging changes in education in England and Wales. Comparable changes were introduced in Scotland and Northern Ireland, which have separate educational systems. A major strand of this reform was the implementation of a national curriculum and national assessment programme.

For each subject, the curriculum is enshrined in law: statutory orders describe the matters, skills and processes to be taught as 'programmes of study' and the knowledge, skills and understanding as 'attainment targets' (ATs) which pupils are expected to have reached at certain stages of schooling. The stages are defined as Key Stage 1 (ages 5–7), 2 (7–11), 3 (11–14) and 4 (14–16).

The ATs are articulated at a series of ten levels. The series of levels is designed to enable progression: most pupils of 7+ are expected to be at level 2 in the system, while most pupils of 11 + are predicted to be at level 4, and so on. The ATs are articulated at each of the ten levels by a series of criteria or statements of attainment which form the basic structure of a criterion-referenced assessment system.

The national assessment programme as outlined in the report of the Task Group on Assessment and Testing (TGAT 1988) and the statutory orders, requires that pupils be assessed against all the ATs by their teachers and on some ATs by external tests called Standard Assessment Tasks (SATs) at the ages of 7, 11 and 14. At these ages the results are combined and must be reported towards the end of that school year. (At 16 the external test is to be the General Certificate of Secondary Education (GCSE) which is currently taken by approximately 85% of the age group, and the grading system of the GCSE is to be merged with the ten-level National Curriculum scale.) Teachers may make their own assessments in any way they wish, but observation, regular informal assessment and keeping examples of work are all encouraged. The results of individual pupils are confidential to themselves, their parents and teachers; results for a class as a whole and a school as a whole are to be available to the parents; results at school level are to be publicly reported.

National Assessment in Primary Schools (NAPS) is an ESRC-funded research project based jointly at the University of London Institute of Education and at King's College, London. The aim of the project is to monitor the implementation of the new national assessment system, together with the interpretation and use of results. Our focus is on teachers' developing assessment practice and therefore we were particularly interested in how the teacher assessment (TA) element of the national assessment programme was carried out. This chapter focuses on TA at Key Stage 1, in the second year of the statutory implementation of national assessment.

Given the emphasis on TA in the TGAT model, one might have expected the Department for Education to initiate a major pro-gramme of in-service training and resource materials to support TA. However, it became clear that the policy of government and the School Examinations and Assessment Council (SEAC) was to give increased weight to the results of the external SATs, leaving teachers with little support in arriving at their own assessments. While SEAC devoted considerable resources to SAT development, the only publications (SEAC, 1990) devoted to teacher assessment (packs A, B and C) were produced rapidly and with insufficient trialling. Both our study and other evaluators (see, for example, Whetton *et al.* 1991) have demonstrated that they proved of little value to class teachers.

Since teachers were largely left alone to implement TA, with in general only a minimal input from their local education authority advisers (Bennett *et al.* 1992), it was clearly an interesting question as to what methods would be selected, and on what implicit or explicit beliefs these would be based.

As the following section will make clear, our attempts in 1991 to elicit detailed, explicit accounts of how teachers made their assessments failed. We realized that much of the teachers' practice was implicit and that the standard research techniques of interview and observation were not adequate to render these activities explicit. We therefore developed a different technique which, together with an interview, and supported by observations of case-study teachers and their earlier interviews, allowed us to develop and describe models of assessment practice used by Year 2 (age 7) teachers. These models appear to reflect beliefs about the nature of teaching and learning in young children.

Gathering data on teacher assessment

Our fieldwork is based on detailed work with Year 2 teachers in each of 32 schools. These are drawn from four local education authorities which were chosen to represent a range of different settings, both socioeconomic and geographic: a northeastern county, a southeastern shire, a London borough and a Midlands metropolitan borough. Both of the last two have substantial numbers of pupils whose first language is not English. Within each school district we have chosen a stratified random sample of eight schools, to include infant, junior, primary, Church of England, Roman Catholic and non-church, and a range of sizes and locations.

Six of the 32 schools, including at least one from each of the four LEAs, were selected for more detailed case study on the basis of illustrating practices which appeared to differ in significant ways.

The data-gathering concerned explicitly with TA has involved: visits to all 32 schools to interview heads and Year 2 teachers about TA (spring 1991); four consecutive days in each of the six case-study schools, focusing on TA methods (autumn 1991); visits to the 25 case-study and non-case-study schools, where the Year 2 teacher had not changed from last year using the 'quote sort' activity to focus on TA (spring 1992); and a postal questionnaire sent to all Year 2 teachers about their 1992 experiences of TA (and SATs) – vignettes of our TA models were sent to all Year 2 teachers as a validation of our observations. (Additional visits were made to schools in both years to gather data about the use of SATs.)

In the 1991 interviews we found teachers unable to describe their TA practices in any detail. Many of the interviews yielded vague descriptions of collecting evidence and details of recordkeeping and planning:

> I keep a folder for each child with pieces of work, a bit of this, a bit of that, as you go along.

> I looked at my notebook, my lists, the children's books and exercise books. From that I could work out their level.

In order to obtain more specific information we included in the following year's fieldwork four days of observation in each of the six case-study schools, focusing on TA. These visits still yielded little observable evidence of TA. Teachers found it difficult to describe precisely what they used to determine the level of attainment and how they reached this decision. Even where teachers claimed that they used ATs, it was not clear how they had done so. One teacher's method of assessing English, for example, was to look at two or three exercise books from one child, 'refer to the Attainment Target' and assign a level.

A way of eliciting more explicit information about their views and practices was therefore needed. For 1992 we developed a sorting activity based on the extraction of quotations about TA which were selected from those made by teachers in our 1991 interviews. Rather than conducting the 'quote sort' as a questionnaire using a Likert scale, we used the activity as a basis for interview, allowing us to combine both qualitative and quantitative methods. This method involved sorting 16 quotes (see Appendix 3.1 for details) into 'like me' or 'not like me' categories. After the teachers had sorted the quotes we had a detailed interview, asking each of them to explain the reasons for the categorization. Altogether, 25 Year 2 teachers were involved: seven from the six case-study schools (one school had a pair of teachers working as a team) and 18 from the non-case-study schools where the Year 2 teacher had not changed between 1991 and 1992.

As a result of this, we have identified three models, or 'ideal types', which vary along the dimensions of *systematicness, integration with teaching* and *ideological underpinning*. We emphasize that the models are not hierarchical in value and that no particular set of views or practices is intended to represent a desired model of TA. Indeed, our informal judgement suggests that there are teachers within each of the groups whose pupils have both relatively high and relatively low standards of attainment.

Although there were some minor difficulties in using authentic quotes (such as confusion resulting from negatives in the wording and the inclusion of more than one idea within the same quote), the teachers engaged with the activity and we were able to analyse their responses. The data from the quote-sort activity and the detailed diagnostic interviews was analysed at several levels. First, a simple count was made of the number of teachers agreeing with each statement (see Appendix 3.2). Then a matrix was drawn up of teachers who agreed with each other in particular quotes. The final quantitative approach was to produce clusters of teachers using the cluster analysis utility on the Datadesk statistical package for the Apple Macintosh. The detailed interview material was analysed using the constant comparative method (Glaser and Strauss 1967) to produce groups of teachers with similar approaches/profiles. These groupings were matched against both the clusters and our classroom observations of these teachers. The first tentative models were refined several times by the project team.

Three models emerged: 'intuitives', 'evidence gatherers' and 'systematic planners'. These models emerged from the analysis of all the data gathered from Year 2 teachers during the first two phases of the project (interviews, classroom observation, quote-sort activity and related interview, review of records and record-keeping practices, accounts of curriculum planning and detailed descriptions of how levels were arrived at for one child).

Preliminary validation of the models was carried out by presentation to a group of LEA advisers, who were not in the NAPS sample;

the models were recognized and endorsed. Further validation was obtained from presenting the models in the form of vignettes (see Appendix 3.3) to our sample of Year 2 teachers. Teachers were asked to choose the vignette which most closely resembled their own practice in order to establish to what extent the descriptions matched their own perceptions. Vignettes seemed an appropriate format to feed back to teachers, as they enabled us to present the essentials of each model, including both behaviour and philosophy, in everyday language with which teachers could identify. They also had the advantage of being brief, which would contribute to the likelihood of response. The wording of each model was considered carefully and we also took care to present the models in an order which was not clearly hierarchical.

Response to the vignettes was requested from all Year 2 teachers we had been dealing with in our 31 sample schools. (One school had withdrawn from the study following the appointment of a new head.) Altogether 31 Year 2 teachers from 24 schools responded to the vignettes, of which 18 were the original Year 2 teachers from the previous year, who had done the quote sort and with whom we were familiar. The remaining 13 teachers were mostly unknown to us, although some had been interviewed or observed for reasons other than the quote sort. Teachers gave us no feedback that the models were unrealistic or that it was difficult to choose one to identify with. Seven teachers did not return a vignette for reasons apparently unconnected with the task, such as resignation, retirement or school closure.

These responses to the vignettes also provided a partial validation of the TA models in the sense that 31 teachers were prepared to commit themselves to a model, thereby recognizing and being able to identify with the models in practice. Furthermore, of the 18 teachers who both did the quote-sort activity and responded to the vignettes, 11 chose the model which we had felt best matched their practice from the data we had available. The extent of the overlap is further validation of the models; we had not expected a complete match since we were aware that the teachers' perceptions of their assessment practice sometimes differed from our descriptions of their practice, based in turn on our own perceptions. In any case, when real teachers are compared with 'ideals', there is rarely a perfect fit (see, for example, MacDonald 1974). Since the models represent 'ideal types', it will not always be possible to place a particular individual squarely within one of them, nor are the types themselves completely distinct.

The models of teacher assessment

The three models of teacher assessment are described below. For two of the models – intuitives and systematic planners – we feel we have identified two fairly distinct sub-groups: the former can be divided into *children's needs ideologists* and *tried and tested methodologists*; the latter into *systematic assessors* and *systematic integrators*. The names were chosen by the team to represent what we felt to be the best summary of the characteristics of each group.

Model I: intuitives

We have termed the teachers in this group 'intuitives' because they object to the imposed system of national assessment as a disruption to intuitive ways of working. Intuitives fall into two sub-groups: the first, 'children's needs ideologists', show a great deal of confidence and can articulate arguments about assessment which defend a child-centred view of curriculum, teaching and learning; the second, 'tried and tested methodologists', feel secure in modes of teaching and assessing practised before the ERA but are less confident in articulating what these are or their actual basis or uses for teaching or assessment purposes. All of the intuitive group of teachers are minimal adopters of national assessment procedures. The children's needs ideologists resist criterion referencing as being in tension with 'whole-child' philosophy and are often confidently critical of the SAT tasks as being inappropriate and ill-matched to their own ideas of 'levelness'. The tried and tested methodologists resist the whole notion of ongoing recorded TA because it means a radical change in behaviour for them:

You are either teaching or assessing, you can't be doing both.

However, they are prepared to carry out SATs following the letter of the law because the materials and instructions are provided and this is a type of assessment familiar to them, being test-like and summative. Thus their resistance to change can be seen to derive partly from their view of teaching, but also partly from the still prevailing traditional 'culture' of assessment noted in Chapters 1 and 2 of this volume.

For all intuitives, there was a reliance on memory and a lack of observable ongoing TA, and thus we were unable to describe in detail the processes that this group were using to make assessments. Teachers themselves spoke about TA in general terms, without reference to statements of attainment:

> Sitting on my own at night when it's nice and quiet and the children have gone home, I looked through what I had for the child, I called on my memory, plans I'd made for what we'd covered, and looked in their folders at the relevant documentation.

One of the main characteristics of this whole group is their rejection of systematic recorded TA, which is seen as interference with real teaching.

> I just can't bear the thought of breaking off to give them a tick. To be honest, in my classroom, I can't keep breaking off and writing things down.

A systematic approach to assessment is criticized as being 'too formal', 'clinical', 'too structured – down such tramlines', and there seems to be a particular dislike of 'the clipboard syndrome' or going around recording all the time.

The children's needs ideologists find it 'too hard to sit back and let a child struggle' without offering some input 'because it's second nature'. They prefer a holistic approach, seeing teaching and assessment taking place simultaneously and 'recording mentally all the time while watching the processes a child is going through'. These teachers subscribe to an 'exploratory' view of learning (Rowland 1987) since they initially guide the task to a point where children can be left to arrive at their own solutions to the problem as jointly defined. They prefer the role of 'provider of a stimulating environment' to that of 'instructor'.

Not surprisingly, devising a list of teacher's questions as an assessment technique 'ignores what the child is saying back to you' and focused observation-based note-taking may even be seen as 'damaging' because 'children are left alone and their concentration breaks down'. Curriculum planning is based on what teachers feel are the needs of children and this means there is no need to have internalized either ATs or statements of attainment because 'you can't always follow what you, the teacher, intend to do'. They would stress the importance of combining an individual conference with each child together with their own reflections on the 'whole' child, before making any final recorded assessment.

The tried and tested methodologists believe you cannot be teaching and assessing simultaneously and seem to base their practice on a sequential understanding that they assess what they have taught. This practice is underpinned by a didactic model of learning (Rowland 1987) in which the teacher defines the child's needs and provides the appropriate instruction. The child responds and the teacher marks and provides feedback. Because the focus is on teaching, they feel that 'you can't record on *ad hoc* assessments you make' so assessment for this group of teachers tends to be summative, taking the form of giving worksheets, scrutinizing tangible evidence like pages of maths from exercise books and doing verbal checks of a child's knowledge by 'getting them on their own and having a little chat about it'. At the end of half terms or terms, they call up their memory and feel that 'if you're worth the name of teacher, you should know your children inside out and be able to recall what children can do'.

In carrying out these summative assessments, intuitives retain and report the value of assessment procedures with which they are familiar such as 'ILEA Checkpoints', teacher-made worksheets and tests, maths worksheets related to published schemes. This is in spite of the fact that the results do not relate to the statements of attainment which form the basis for TA under the National Curriculum.

Teachers' close knowledge (often rooted in long careers in teaching) is the main basis on which tried and tested methodologists in particular make their assessments. There is a strong belief that 'the assessing needs to be done by the actual class teacher' and not someone else; teachers have got to *know* a child to know whether 'what they have done on paper' is good or not or in order 'to know if the result is really amazing for that child'. Consequently previous records are not observed to be readily available or consulted and teachers rely mainly on their own personal judgements. Planning based on diagnostic assessment was not observed in their classrooms, rather there was a tendency to 'all start at the same beginning point and then spread out'.

These teachers often have their own implicit standards; for example, in relation to the SAT tasks:

> That was no way a level 3 task. You have to do more to get a level 3. We know what quality work is.

Because of these implicitly held notions of levels of difficulty and ability, intuitives resist criterion referencing, relying rather on 'gut reaction', and an all-round close knowledge of children built up after spending so much time with them. Close knowledge involves children's 'everyday performance, personality, the way they present themselves, their acquisition of knowledge outside of school' and their interactions within groups. This is used as a basis for recording assessment:

> I don't think I can discount what I know about a child from its attainment.

> You have to take account of contextual issues because that's what being a professional is.

Some found it hard to ignore children's attitudes and behaviour when recording attainment, particularly on SATs:

> If a child had really tried hard and put a lot of effort in it, it's very hard not to give it [the NC level] to them.

And allowances were made for age:

> It's so unfair: one of the August birthdays is quite a bright little boy. He just hasn't got there yet. So I feel like giving him a little more leeway.

Because teachers continue to include all these biographical and contextual details and do not 'distil' out attainment when assessing children, one can say that they are passive resisters of the criterion referenced system characteristic of the national assessment model.

Of all the teachers in the sample, this group have made least adaptation to their preferred ways of working. The ideologists bitterly resent change imposed from outside (Cooper 1988), wanting to protect 'the human face of teaching' and their personal investment in it (Nias 1989), and worry that shifting to a focus on assessment could cause damage to children. This 'moral accountability' felt by primary teachers was noted in a comparative study by Broadfoot and Osborn (1986). Collegiality in the schools from which they come has provided them with considerable confidence in their practices and beliefs, which enables them to resist the pressures to change.

Change can threaten to invalidate long years of experience (Marris 1975) and some long-serving tried and tested methodologists express a strong reluctance to accept the national assessment model:

> I haven't memorized the ATs – they're going to change anyway. I find the jargon difficult.

There is among some of this group a sense of insecurity, often related to lack of personal support within their schools. They report a fear of 'sinking under paper' and an uneasiness with constant educational change, the last few years seeming like

> the Aldershot Assault Course. No sooner do you get over one wall when another looms up.

As one in a long line of recent changes, National Curriculum assessment requires teachers to engage in more detailed work plans and give more attention to techniques which will support criterion referencing for individual pupils. The perceived amount of energy and time required to learn the new skills and roles associated with the innovation has provided a rationale for resistance within this group (House 1974).

Model EG: *evidence gatherers*

These teachers have a basic belief in the primacy of teaching, rather than assessing. Their main method of assessment relies on collecting evidence which they only later evaluate. They have gone some way towards adapting the requirements of national assessment and they could be considered rational adapters, in the sense that they have adapted in such a way as to not change their teaching: collecting evidence does not interfere with teaching practice. Evidence gathering is associated with a belief that pupils generally learn what is taught and only what is taught; thus assessment follows teaching in order to check that the process is going according to plan.

One of the main characteristics of evidence gatherers, therefore, is that assessment is accommodated within existing systems and it is not always planned in:

> I don't really plan a task to cover assessment. I plan first what I want to do and then see how it can be fitted into assessment.

The teachers in this group do not often plan assessment activities, but rely on assessment 'opportunities' to arise within their normal classroom teaching:

> You think, 'Oh, that's another Attainment Target'.

This system is dependent on the teacher's ability to recognize tasks which can be 'matched' to the national assessment ATs and to 'vaguely have assessment in mind all the time'. Having recognized an activity as usable for assessment, the teacher then devises a means of gathering evidence:

> A piece of work we did on autumn days, we got to talking about that and a lot of science points came out of it . . . so, quickly we do a weather chart! They covered all the other things really well and it was obvious from the discussion, but we just had to have the weather chart for evidence.

Teachers tend to think in terms of ATs, rather than statements of attainment, and the 'matching' of tasks to ATs usually takes place after the activity itself, either at the end of the day or at the end of term when recording is done:

> I hadn't really planned how this exercise would fit into assessment, but I see now that it does. I will have to look up exactly where and how it fits in . . . I'll look it up in the book when I get home.

Where teachers do plan assessment activities, such assessment is primarily for the purpose of collecting written evidence, rather than for diagnostic assessment:

> I sometimes set up an activity. Quite often the worksheet is part of that, to prove they can do it.

Evidence is gathered in relation to the ATs and the purpose of assessment is largely seen to be proving National Curriculum coverage:

I know that if we cover these topics we'll have done all the ATs. I like things done as part of topic work.

Such planning for assessment typically goes on at the same time as planning topic work, usually before each term. Once topics are chosen, ATs are matched against them, although statements of attainment may also be looked at during this planning level. There is a general confidence that national assessment is being 'covered' within the topic work. This may be either an individual teacher's termly plan, or whole-school topic work as part of a 'rolling programme'. The link between assessment and topic work enables teachers to incorporate assessment into their usual way of doing things, and makes assessment more user-friendly:

It means a lot more to me if it's part of an activity that I'm going to do or part of my topic for the term – to make sure that I'm covering the attainment targets with my topics.

The teacher can identify 'gaps' in the curriculum at the time she records on her assessment record sheets, which is usually done termly in the school holidays.

When you go through and fill in the record sheets you can look at them and just find a little point that you haven't covered, so you make a little note that you have to do this.

Overall, a programme of planned topic work is seen to ensure that both national assessment and National Curriculum have been done.

Not surprisingly, given the title of this model, there is an emphasis on gathering evidence of all kinds:

I keep everything. I'm known as a hoarder.

The main characteristic of this group is the need to gather evidence in abundance, with an emphasis on written work, which enables the teacher to have 'proof' of what has been done. 'Trying to get as much evidence as I can' is the aim of many of these teachers (and may preclude the value of the assessment itself). 'Getting the result down on paper' is seen to be essential, because teachers feel accountable and, under national assessment, are concerned that they may be asked to produce evidence of their assessment of children:

I keep a camera in the cupboard for technology. It is the only record you've got if somebody asked you for evidence.

Evidence may be collected from a variety of sources, including pages from workbooks, worksheets from published schemes, teacher-devised worksheets, children's written work, spelling tests, observation and questioning children on work they have done. There is a heavy reliance on worksheets and maths schemes as written evidence, though teachers tend not to trust such schemes to cover the ATs adequately:

> I've yet to see a scheme which has gone into National Curriculum adequately or entirely. Worksheets can support, yes, but that shouldn't be the system by itself. Schemes miss things out, so assessment based on this will miss things out.

> Our Nuffield maths scheme, I have put the attainment targets alongside. Nuffield did produce a sheet that did that but I produced a sheet that verified it.

Teachers therefore devise their own worksheets to complement the published schemes:

> I still give my own maths tests to cover Scottish Primary Maths. I would never go by just what they have done on the worksheets or in the book. I would want to be sure.

Most of the teachers in this group acknowledge that 'you don't always have a piece of recorded work every time' and that other kinds of evidence, including teachers' notes on observations, may be valid:

> I set activities and watch them and then we work on worksheets as well as see what they've done. But the outcome is not just the worksheet, I have assessed the whole process.

> I would never rely all on my memory. You must have it backed up with evidence. You've got to have your notes as evidence.

Another key feature of evidence gathering is that assessments are summative, rather than formative in nature:

> I would just write it down but I wouldn't go into records until I am ready to record. I leave assessing to the end of term.

Recording assessment is usually done termly, when evidence is gathered in one place and the teacher reflects on the work the child has done over the term:

If I have their pieces of work there I can just sit there and think 'this particular child has achieved that'.

Most, though not all, of the teachers in this group prefer not to rely on memory because

you couldn't possibly call up your memory on each child's performance on every AT – it's just too difficult.

The 'bits and bobs of evidence' which are 'pulled together for the end of term' enable the teacher to sit and reflect on the child's achievements over the term and 'weigh up' performance overall. Despite the emphasis on collecting evidence, though, not all the evidence that has been collected will be used in the awarding of levels and it is possible that in some cases evidence is used selectively to support the teacher's intuition.

Another characteristic of evidence gatherers is that there is an increased awareness of national assessment procedures and, in some cases, a degree of excitement brought on by new developments:

We do observations all the time in the class, we're getting quite familiar with this sort of assessment. Initially you're dying to offer them a bit of help or advice but not now: now I can quite happily sit down and just write down what I see.

The teachers themselves are conscious of their increased awareness of assessment procedures since the implementation of national assessment. Overall, assessment for these teachers is a new and higher priority, although they are not prepared to let it become 'the be-all and end-all', as they are anxious to keep as many of their former ways of working as can be retained within new assessment and curriculum procedures.

The teachers tend not to have internalized the statements of attainment and they do not interrogate the evidence in a systematic way, although they have familiarity with the ATs and are able to recognize how activities fit into them:

This activity is AT4 or 5. So I've already got that in mind, but I wouldn't have done this time last year.

They are also much more aware of levels:

You're aware of the level already, even when you first look at what they have made.

> I have a particular awareness of Year 3 children this year as level 3 last year.

Their awareness extends to assessment techniques, where observation and children's talk are recognized as increasingly important for assessment:

> You constantly talk to children and now you're more aware of what they say in response because you've got this in your mind all the time: do they understand what they are talking about? There is a new awareness about the responses.

The teachers have also developed an understanding of the distinction of attainment from other contextual factors such as effort and behaviour, although some admit that this is sometimes hard to accept:

> It is very difficult sometimes to stay unbiased, but one has to. We mustn't let the child's behaviour cloud our thinking.

> Obviously you know the children and what they have put into it, but you still have to keep separate what they can actually *do*. It's not always easy but you have to do it.

Some teachers in this group feel that although attainment is clearly separate from other factors ('effort does not equal attainment'), new assessment procedures require the teacher to suppress what she knows about the 'whole child':

> Before SATs it was the whole child that you were really looking at. Now you still know the whole child but on paper you can only put what they actually do.

It appears that while the teachers are newly aware of the notion of criterion referencing, there are times when contextual factors must be taken into account:

> If you know a child is in some sort of bother, you've got to look at assessment against this context. So if a child has underachieved because of certain circumstances, you wouldn't accept the assessment without considering this.

> If I have given a child a high level all the times before, I will leave that level. I won't change it, because I know what the child is capable of.

A final feature of the evidence gathering model is that systematic assessment is seen as a threat to relationships with children. The teachers in this group had a fear of national assessment interfering with their relationships with children if they were to 'go over the top' by adopting more systematic assessment practices. Assessing against a can-do list was seen as 'tabulated' and 'judgemental', as well as unnecessarily systematic:

> We haven't broken it down into a can-do list but I think in our minds we know what the children can do because we're observing all the time.

There was also concern that the can-do list might put some children at a disadvantage because either the teacher might be 'missing something' or

> some children might never get on to it because they can't do the things on the can-do list.

Although one teacher kept a list of the ATs and statements of attainment in her handbag and referred to them every week when doing her lesson plans, carrying such a list was seen as interfering with the 'real job' of teaching:

> You'd never get on with your work if you were doing that.

> I feel this is more or less teaching through ATs or statements of attainment.

Similarly, recording or note-taking on the spot was seen sceptically and acceptable only 'providing you just jot it down and don't make a thing of it'. While some teachers acknowledged that recording on the spot was more accurate than reflecting back, they did not see it as a priority and had not incorporated it into their own assessment practice:

> I'm sure it is much more accurate but I just can't find the time to do it.

Finally, some evidence gatherers clearly rejected such practices as note-taking on the spot:

> I think if you are taking notes while you are making candles, you're in for trouble.

Overall, evidence gatherers shared concerns with their critical intuitive colleagues in rejecting the methods of systematic assessors. Rather than rely on memory and intuition for assessment, however, they favoured gathering evidence and then reflecting back over the child's performance during the term in a summative manner.

Their new awareness of national assessment procedures and their willingness to adapt were perceived as accounting for National Curriculum coverage and therefore assessment was accommodated within existing systems, rather than making major changes to their habitual teaching roles.

Model SP: systematic planners

We have called the third group of teachers 'systematic planners'. Planning time specifically for assessment has become part of their practice (although this varies in the degree to which it is integrated with everyday teaching) and the planned assessment of groups and individuals informs future task design and classwork. A constructivist approach to learning underpins this model, with teachers expecting children to learn in idiosyncratic ways; they are willing to try children on higher levels not yet taught, using such opportunities diagnostically. Such teachers also demonstrate social constructivist beliefs (Pollard 1987) in that they attach importance to interacting and arriving at shared meanings, both with pupils and with their fellow professionals in the context of TA. These teachers have embraced the national assessment requirements and understand the principles of criterion referencing, often breaking down statements of attainment into smaller steps. While upholding the importance of teaching, they report real value in continuous diagnostic assessment as an enhancement to their effectiveness:

> I need to know that at a particular time of day, I am actually going to be assessing one thing. You've got to be structured, you've got to know what you are looking for.

The most significant characteristic of this group of teachers is that they plan for assessment on a systematic basis. This means that the teacher consciously devotes some part of the school week to assessing, and explicitly links the results of assessment and curriculum planning.

There are two identifiable sub-groups in this category. Some teachers, whom we have called 'systematic assessors', give *daily* concentrated time to one group of children at a time and have devised systems to lessen demands made upon them by the rest of the class. Some teachers wear badges or put up a 'busy flag' as a sign they are not to be interrupted. These teachers often make it clear that it is quite permissible to ask peers, not the teacher, for help or they devise an agenda of tasks for the children to work through.

Other teachers, whom we have called 'systematic integrators', do not separate themselves off from the rest of the class but circulate, gathering evidence in different ways which feeds into *weekly* recorded assessment and informs planning. The clearest example of this occurs in the case of two teachers working as a pair and sharing 60 children. They collect assessment data on children throughout the week and have devised a 'Friday sheet' on which is recorded (after consideration and interpretation of each other's comments) their jointly agreed assessments of children. Also on this sheet there will be an agreed plan for children's subsequent work. Thus a cyclical programme develops.

However, in spite of these differences, the two groups of systematic planners have much in common and the remaining descriptions apply to both groups. For all systematic planners assessment is diagnostic:

> You're making some assessment of previous work because you have to assess in order to teach . . . whether they are ready to go on to the next stage.

Children are selected on the basis of previously recorded assessment. The process becomes cyclical. Diagnostic assessment feeds into planning for individual, group and class activities which, in turn, offer opportunities for more diagnostic assessment. Records are generally accessible and used. However, these teachers are often willing to try children 'on the next level' without necessarily teaching first. For example, following on from what two children had attained previously, they were asked to order numbers to 1000. The teacher left them alone to do this. The task was not presented as a maths 'exercise' but rather as a problem-solving task to be recorded informally. The teacher spent some time in discussion with the children: 'I just want to see how you experiment with this.' She could see the kind of errors one child was making and gave some help. She also took their papers home that evening. Her plan was:

> I'll look through the sheets. I'm going to get Pam to do some more work. I might make her a worksheet. I'll think it out when I go home.

Pam was not given a worksheet next day but the teacher devoted a planned amount of time to working with her.

By giving children work at the next level without specifically teaching first, assessment seems less 'bolted on' to teaching and becomes a learning process for teachers.

> The interesting thing about teacher assessments are that they surprise you.

For this group of teachers assessment techniques are multiple and children are assessed both formatively and summatively through a combination of: observation; open-ended questioning (the questions varying from child to child); teacher–pupil discussion; running records; and scrutiny of classwork. Attention is paid to fitting the assessment technique to the activity being assessed. One of the significant differences between this model and the other two is the sharp focus on statements of attainment. Teachers' self-devised checklists are used, often comprising lists of 'can-do' indicators which represent the teacher's analysis and interpretation of each of the statements of attainment, broken down further into descriptions of what a child might say or do to demonstrate attainment:

> Even with the statements of attainment, there are still smaller steps. Like, the statement of attainment says 'know number facts to 10'. But the steps before that in basic addition – there are all sorts of ways of going about that.

Teachers may assess more than one statement of attainment at a time, perhaps a 'process one and a content one', but these will be planned and not simply noticed in passing (although serendipitous observations of a child's knowledge or understanding are not ignored). Because of the multiple methods in use, evidence of attainment for the final record takes many forms:

> The record would be a drawing together of everything. It would be based on 'can-dos', children's own records, their spontaneous comments and observations.

In addition to the above reported list, critical incidents both noted and memorized, annotated pieces of work, annotated photographs and worksheets 'used for consolidation' may be used.

Unlike the intuitives, relying solely on memory is thought to be untrustworthy:

> I don't think memory is accurate enough. I think that's when you assume things about children.

and note-taking and recording at the time on self-designed formats are favoured:

> We keep boxes of sticky labels at our sides during most activities and we record as we go along or at the end of a session but not at the end of a day, because its difficult to remember.

One piece of tangible evidence (particularly one published work-card) or one session of observation is thought to be insufficient evidence of attainment because

> you're teaching to the worksheet, you could be missing out chunks. That's not developing children.

In addition, teachers like to have some ownership of the assessment process:

> I suppose assessment to me is something special . . . I tend to put a little more effort into it myself. I don't use the published workcards.

Teachers may 'revisit' the statements of attainment several times 'to really say if they have attained it', so as 'not [to] push and give a false picture' and may repeat assessments over time often using different techniques 'to double-check, be fair' or 'do a quick stock-take'.

These teachers have now become very familiar with national assessment procedures, have internalized the ATs and statements of attainment or have them permanently displayed for easy reference, either on planning sheets or on assessment proformas they have made. They can often quote them when assessing by observation or recognize national assessment levels when looking at a piece of work:

> I think when I'm marking say English 3, it leaps up from the page . . . 'Ah, this is a level 2'.

Systematic planners separate attainment from other factors and are able to 'distil' attainment in the National Curriculum from other aspects of a child's achievement; they prefer to record attainment separately from attitudinal, contextual and biographical details, although these also may be recorded, sometimes within a school policy of records of achievement (ROA). The effort a child makes is not what counts. It is the result that is important:

> You must be quite specific about what a child has attained. The effort goes into ROA. You make notes of it in other places but not in teacher assessment.

> When a particularly difficult child was being teacher-assessed, the teacher might be thinking about his general problems in the classroom. We've found that using the criteria, this child, being assessed on exactly the same thing as everyone else, has actually shown he's doing quite well.

Such teachers have therefore internalized and are using a criterion-referenced model of assessment.

Systematic planners are not resistant to the new methods of assessment imposed by central government. They see systematic diagnostic assessment as adding to their professionalism:

> I think some teachers get hung up on the word 'assessment' and get frightened by it and they undervalue what they are really doing.

They reject the trial-and-error methods and intuitive guessing of the other two groups, stressing that they have teaching in mind but:

> teaching based on assessment done sometime earlier. The greatest thing is to make notes so it informs your teaching.

They do not reject the notion that the child is at the heart of the learning process, nor that the 'whole child' is important:

> I use my knowledge of the child in my *approach* to teaching and assessing but not in my actual assessment.

Of all teachers in the sample, these teachers have made the most progress towards a hypothetical integrated model of teacher assessment. It could be that their own practice before the ERA was bound by particular systems of organization and classroom management (for example, the methods favoured by 'group instructors' and 'rotating changers' described by Galton *et al.* 1980) and hence was more amenable to the adoption of systematic assessment.

However, the balance of incentives seems, for this group, to outweigh the disincentives and national assessment has offered them a sense of mastery, excitement and accomplishment (Huberman and Miles 1984). The systems they have devised can be seen as a stage in taking ownership of the innovation, enabling the teachers to retain a feeling of control.

Discussion

Criterion referencing

National assessment is a broadly criterion-referenced model of assessment and is intended to reflect whether or not a child possesses the knowledge, skills and understandings defined by more or less specific criteria (statements of attainment). Criterion referencing represents a new departure for infant teachers, who have previously assessed children in a more normative way, also taking account of contextual factors (such as effort or social background) which may affect a child's performance. We therefore need to consider how the TA models that we have identified address the issue of criterion referencing and to what extent teachers have been prepared to change their former practices in order to embrace this new method of assessment.

A questionnaire sent to Year 2 and Year 3 teachers in autumn 1991 showed that many schools have adopted whole-school record-keeping policies, using records that pass up the school with each child. While the majority of this recording is done at statement of attainment level, our observations revealed that only one group of teachers were using criterion referencing on statements of attainment as part of their classroom practice. This is supported by Her Majesty's Inspectorate (1992), observing that 'few teachers used specific criteria matched to attainment against National Curriculum levels in their day to day marking'.

Across two of the models (evidence gatherers and intuitives), teachers made infrequent or no reference to statements of attainment; this was possibly because of the summative ways of recording at the end of terms. Intuitives, particularly, rejected notions of criterion-referenced assessment by continuing to incorporate effort or background factors when making an assessment, and by their refusal to internalize or make readily available the statements of attainment.

These groups, rather than using statements of attainment, tended to have an overall notion of 'levelness' and therefore relied on implicit norms in relation to ranking children:

From what I know of Debbie, she just isn't a Level 3 child.

The quasi-norm-referenced use of level 3 to indicate children of well above average attainment caused some teachers to ignore or ridicule the possibility of children reaching level 4, although our observations in a few schools, not always in affluent areas, demonstrated that pupils were able to achieve level 4 in some aspects of the SATs.

The more systematic of the systematic planners carried out criterion referencing by use of a 'can-do' list against which children are assessed. This list originated from the statements of attainment themselves, which had been interpreted and broken down into simpler and more specific can-do statements so that criterion referencing could be more easily integrated into classroom practice. (The ongoing use of criterion-referenced assessment starting from rather broadly defined criteria raises problems of reliability because of possibly differing interpretations by teachers; this issue is discussed in other chapters.) Some systematic planners, in order to carry out frequent or spontaneous assessment had memorized statements of attainment, or carried a list of the statements with them, showing that criterion referencing was both clearly understood and being used in practice.

Overall, though, there is little evidence so far that teachers have widely accepted criterion referencing, or that they are about to do so. Ideological or logistic objections, as described in the intuitive and to a lesser extent, in the evidence gathering models, are preventing them from moving away from normative ways of assessing into the criterion-referenced model prescribed by national assessment.

Use of results for formative purposes

Results passed up to intuitives and evidence gatherers were used as general guidelines only and not used as a basis for planning class-work or forming groups. More systematic teachers used 'inherited' results to inform them of children's attainment on the National Curriculum and thus to place them in attainment groups.

The degree to which the groups of teachers used assessment results for formative purposes varied, with intuitives and evidence gatherers retaining their previous patterns of teaching and prefer-ring a more summative role for teacher assessment. Systematic integrators, however, incorporated formative assessment into their weekly forecasts of work, while systematic planners used assess-ment to feed into individual and class planning on a daily basis.

Models of teaching and learning

From our interviews and observations of the teachers, we are able to get some indication of their views of how children learn, which links, of course, with their preferred style of teaching.

Although intuitives as a group had a child-centred view of cur-riculum, teaching and learning, the children's needs ideologists subscribe to an exploratory or scaffolded view of learning, where they provide a stimulating environment and guide the child to the point at which they feel that the child can carry out the task on his or her own; while the tried and tested methodologists have a more didactic model of learning, where the teacher herself decides on the child's needs and provides the appropriate instruction. Evidence gatherers similarly tend to believe that pupils learn what is taught and only what is taught. The systematic planners, on the other hand, have a constructivist approach to learning: they expect children to learn in idiosyncratic ways, and not necessarily what is taught; they also believe in arriving at shared meanings with pupils.

This information on learning was collected, not specifically, but as a by-product of the work on TA; it is therefore rather skeletal and we aim to develop this aspect of our research in the future.

Conclusions

Teacher assessment of the National Curriculum has been particularly difficult for infant teachers because of the lack of training and support materials.

In Northern Ireland teachers have a range of materials called External Assessment Resources which they can use when they wish to support their assessments. The resources are listed in a catalogue and schools may select three per subject. Provision of material such as this would have helped teachers in England in getting to grips with TA (see also Torrance 1991a, for a discussion of this possibility). Of course, the provision of assessment resources to support TA might serve to encourage a style of TA as mini-SAT, always external to the teaching process, a practice which Harlen and Qualter (1991) warn against. Our view, however, is that for many teachers a stage of doing mini-external assessments is just that – a stage – and that as their confidence and experience develops they move on to more informal, integrated, truly formative assessment.

With no offered model of TA it is perhaps not surprising that our teachers came up with a range of approaches. These approaches were related to their espoused views of teaching and learning, their general style of organization and their reaction to the imposition of the National Curriculum and its assessment. They were thus developing assessment practice in line with their general practice and philosophy of primary education. That it should have happened in this way is not surprising. What is particularly interesting to us as researchers is the relationship between teaching, learning and assessment in the teachers' practice; the link between assessment and learning is a crucial one but is not generally widely addressed.

Important, too, is what these teachers are telling us about criterion-referenced assessment. Evidence supporting this reluctance to assess on an overly analytical basis comes also from Year 3 teachers who received the national assessment information along with the Year 2 children who came up to them in September 1991 and 1992. Some of these teachers wanted *more than objective* test results, they wanted subjective information about children which was, they feared, being downgraded in the national assessment programme. Consulting with the previous teacher and looking together at children's work offered an opportunity to look at the whole child; no amount of hard data on a form could replace this activity. Despite its place as a major theme in the development of educational assessment, attempts to develop criterion-referenced assessment from the top have not been particularly successful in the past (Black and Dockrell 1984; Pennycuick and Murphy 1988; Brown 1989). If the philosophy of criterion-referenced assessment does not fit with strongly held philosophies of infant education, then we may expect to find resistance to it which will serve to weaken its principles (for example, by arriving at levels through norming and ranking processes).

National and international debate of issues such as these is critical to the continued development of sound assessment practice in schools. We are fortunate to be able to continue our work over the next 3 years and will use some of these same techniques with Key Stage 2 teachers. We hope thus to validate and extend our understanding of TA at Key Stage 1 to teachers of older children and to explore more fully links between assessment practice and assumptions about learning.

Acknowledgement

1 The research reported here was funded by the Economic and Social Research Council, grant reference number 000 23 2192. A version of this chapter first appeared in *Research Papers in Education*, 8(3): 305–27 (1993).

Appendix 3.1   How we used respondents' quotations to focus on teacher assessment

1 Gather all quotes about TA from our phase 1 and phase 2 visits.
2 Select 16 quotes from data on different aspects of TA.
3 Put the quotes on to cards suitable for sorting.
4 Present cards to Year 2 teacher in pilot school for sorting: tape their comments while sorting and record their responses into 'like me', 'not like me' and 'middle' categories.
5 Present cards for sorting to 25 Year 2 teachers.

6 Transcribe tapes in full and organize responses on a sheet for easy reference, i.e. columns of responses under categories.
7 Make tables of 'like me' and 'not like me' from responses.
8 Match teachers who are most and least like each other.
9 Account for differences in responses and assess methodology.
10 Make a cluster analysis.
11 Match quote choices and cluster groups to our models of TA.

Appendix 3.2   Quotes used

Quote	*Number of teachers agreeing out of 25*

A   I try to remain unbiased in my assessments, but I find children's behavioural problems difficult to ignore.   14

B   We have broken down ATs into a can-do list and we observe children against this list.   5

C   There is a lot of oral work in science and I find you can assess English skills through science activities even though the emphasis is on science.   24

D   I don't think I will be able to discount what I know about the child from its attainment. No one can tell the effort behind the result as well as the teacher.   11

E   I look at how it all went, how children approached the task, their attitude, whether they were copying or following the leader, whether they attained or covered.   24

F   For a lot of ATs you can use written work. For some it's a lot of observation and you have to ask them what they've done because it's processes.   25

G   From our maths scheme you can hang quite a lot on the ATs, so I would use those worksheets and I can tell quite a lot through the worksheets.   12

H I set up activities and watch them and once I feel
   they've understood thoroughly, then I give them a
   worksheet. After the worksheet, I assess the outcome
   and award a level.   13

I You observe things and make a note of things that
   just happen. You think, 'Oh, that's another AT'.
   You make a note of these things and at the end of
   the day you put them into your records where
   relevant.   10

J At the end of each term or half term, I call up my
   memory of a child's performance on the AT.   8

K I do a lot of talking to the children to see if they
   exhibit the sort of knowledge that you think fits the
   AT.   24

L I feel that recording at the time is more accurate
   than reflecting back.   15

M I look at a statement of attainment (SOA) and devise
   a small list of questions which will test a child's
   knowledge of that SOA. I put the list into my diary
   and, during the activity, ask all the children in the
   group the same set of questions.   10

N I take a photograph either as a record of work done,
   like when a child has made a model, or as a trigger
   to my own memory. The snap triggers my memory
   back to the questions children were asking or the
   knowledge they were displaying or the way they were
   going about something, like on a field trip when the
   children are involved and enjoying something.   11

O I keep a piece of paper with me with the ATs and
   SOAs clearly written out.   5

P You are either teaching or assessing, you can't be
   doing both.   4

Appendix 3.3   Vignettes

Please tick the model that is MOST like you:

Model A

I prefer to plan the ATs into my topic work and I know that if we cover these topics we'll have done all the ATs. I tend not to plan too many assessment activities because I think one can become too systematic about assessment. I'm quite familiar with the ATs now, which helps me recognize opportunities for assessment.

I think it's very important to gather as much evidence as I can, things like pieces of children's work, worksheets they've done, little notes I have made, anything I have noticed while they are working.

I do my recording at the half term or the end of term when I sit down with all the evidence I have gathered and think about the child's performance. I wouldn't just rely on my memory for that, you have to have it backed up by evidence. I can give them a level using the evidence plus what I remember.

Overall, I prefer to go about my usual teaching and use assessment opportunities as they occur.

Model B

I tend to see assessment as a whole process; it's a part of what teachers do all the time and there is no need to plan it in. I have a general picture of the whole child and what a child can do; this is where the teacher's skills and experience are important.

I prefer assessment to be informal so that spontaneity is not lost. I plan what the children need. I don't have particular ATs or statements of attainment (SOAs) in mind. I'm recording mentally all the time when watching the processes a child is going through. I don't take notes because I think that can interfere with your relationships with children. I might give a worksheet or a little test to check understanding or something I have taught.

As a professional, I think you have to take account of the contextual issues such as attitudes and social background.

When it comes to recording for national assessment, I can reflect on what I know about the child.

Model C

I need to know that at a particular time of day I am actually going to be assessing. I like to be structured and know which SOAs I want to assess. Beforehand, I try to interpret the SOAs and break them down into a kind of can-do list: descriptions of what children might do or say to show they are meeting the National Curriculum criteria. I may assess the same SOA more than once, to double-check and be fair.

I'll observe and question the children while they are working and record at the time or soon afterwards on my own checklists. These notes will inform my future planning because you have to assess in order to teach.

I think you need to be quite specific about what a child has attained on the National Curriculum and record this separately from other things like effort, context and background details; they can be recorded elsewhere, say in a child's record of achievement.

While observing, I am often surprised by what children can do (especially in areas I haven't yet taught) and overall I feel that doing ongoing TA has improved my skills as a teacher.

4

AUTHENTIC ASSESSMENTS IN A COMPETITIVE SECTOR: INSTITUTIONAL PREREQUISITES AND CAUTIONARY TALES

Alison Wolf

Introduction: the UK context

'Authentic' or 'performance' assessments have become generally applauded in recent years, on both sides of the Atlantic: and the arguments in their favour – rehearsed, for example by Resnick and Resnick (1992) – are certainly powerful. This chapter, however, presents some cautionary tales, drawn from the sector of UK education which has embraced this approach most enthusiastically, and draws some more general conclusions about the prospects and perils of authentic assessment. The chapter draws on a number of evaluation and research projects which we have been carrying out over the last few years for the Department of Employment (which has major responsibility for funding vocational and technical education in the UK), including some previously unpublished figures on assessor reliability.

The structure of upper secondary education in Britain differs substantially from that in the USA (or most other European countries). An important component is the further education (FE) sector, encompassing around 700 FE colleges. Further education is post-compulsory (that is, confined to students aged 16 or over), and involves full-time and part-time students, many following evening courses. These colleges do not award degrees, nor do they enroll most of the 16–19-year-old students who intend to go on to university. The main route to higher education in Britain is academic studies leading to final examinations taken at age 17 or 18; and most of the students aiming for these remain in school after the age of 16.

However, this covers only about a third of the age cohort. Increasing numbers of the others stay in full- or part-time education after age 16, but follow other, less traditionally academic courses. Some of these courses are vocational in a highly specific way, designed to provide craft training in, for example, construction or catering – thus apprentices have traditionally spent some of their time off the job studying in further education colleges. More and more of these courses, however, are vocational in only a very broad sense, and are in fact treated by the students concerned as an extension of general education, which does not commit them to a particular trade or occupation. Thus, there has been a huge increase in 'business' or 'tourism studies' courses; and a move to make engineering courses far more general than in the past. All these courses are accredited by national bodies, which have grown up over a long period of time – some confined to a particular area, some offering awards in a wide range of subject and vocational areas, and all dependent on fees from candidates for their survival.

Until recently, FE colleges were part of the local education authorities (LEAs). Now, following recent legislation, they are fully independent incorporated bodies, something which has naturally increased the openness and the importance of competition between them. While their basic source of finance is fees from central government, paid on the basis of full-time enrolments, they also depend heavily on special contracts. Most important of these are contracts from the Department of Employment's local offices for training courses for adult unemployed people, and for 16–18-years-olds on Youth Training Schemes, designed for the lowest-achieving part of the age cohort, and combining work experience with some formal training and education. In this area, the colleges compete head-on with independent training providers, who will most commonly specialize in a particular occupational area (such as construction or hairdressing).

These changes in the institutional framework of FE have taken place alongside major reforms in the assessment and qualification system. The myriad examining and accrediting bodies have not been abolished, but they have all had to reform their awards in line with a national structure for National Vocational Qualifications (NVQs) which attempts to provide greater transparency and coherence by fitting all awards of this type into one of five levels. This reform is overseen by a new government agency, the National Council for Vocational Qualifications (NCVQ). It has developed an exhaustive set of requirements for the new qualifications which have had huge repercussions for classroom practice.

The most important – indeed, the deciding – characteristic of these reforms has been the extent to which they are assessment-led. There are no requirements about length of time on course, teaching methods, resourcing, or indeed any aspects of curriculum except in so far as they are implied by the assessment requirements. However, unlike much of the US discussion of measurement-driven instruction (MDI), whose proponents (see, for example, Popham 1987) apparently envisage compulsory, key elements with large measures of teacher autonomy, in the NVQ system everything is designed to be assessed. In other words, the assessment requirements, although at one level leaving curriculum considerations unshackled, at another are extremely prescriptive. They envisage that every single element of an award will be assessed explicitly, and lay down their requirements accordingly.

The other major characteristics of the NVQ approach are that assessment is criterion-referenced, and that it is performance-based. Since the particular form of criterion referencing adopted for the system has had a major impact on classroom practice, I shall be saying some more about this below: but for the moment I want to concentrate on the performance-based aspect of the requirements.

If we make the conventional distinction between *sample assessment* (direct sampling of the behaviour in which one is interested) and *sign assessment* (testing of something which is assumed to be directly and functionally related to the construct under consideration), it is clear that the architects of NVQs were profoundly suspicious of 'signs'. They saw them as, first of all, simply less valid. They were aware of the literature detailing the limited predictive validity of pencil-and-paper tests for applied skills; and profoundly suspicious of the whole psychometric movement. As one of the main architects of the new system has commented:

> There [are] far too many unnecessary barriers and constraints in . . . gaining qualifications . . . [Vocational education has] tended to be 'educationally' oriented both in content and the values which are implicit in its delivery . . . The educational influence is apparent in the forms of assessment adopted . . . where written and multiple choice tests carry more weight than practical demonstrations. . . . [The result is that] the potential of the majority of individuals has seldom been fulfilled in previous generations.
>
> (Jessup 1991)

The designers of the NVQ system considered themselves to be radicals, breaking down the unnecessary barriers raised by academic self-interest. Too often, they felt, tests which were being used to judge, screen and fail people were testing academic abilities at the expense of those practical accomplishments which were actually relevant to the occupation in question. Moving away from conventional testing to direct performance sampling was considered a major blow for equal opportunities and access. This view found favour with the radical right-wing government of the Thatcher years because the latter had a related agenda. In the vocational and professional area the government also saw traditional examinations as a weapon of sectional self-interest. Apprenticeships were too often associated with 'time-serving': across the board, mysterious and non-transparent tests were used to restrict access. Clarification of performance requirements, and assessment by direct sampling, would break down these barriers and open up to the labour market.

In the early days, NVQ requirements were for performance assessment in the purest sense: direct samples of the sort of 'out-come' behaviour which was desired. Thus, in construction, it was decided that all assessment should take place through practical tasks, in an environment which simulated the workplace as closely as possible. Theoretical papers were unnecessary: knowledge (including ability to carry out the relevant calculations and write up any workplans, invoices, and so on) should all be assessed within the context of either a real or a completely simulated task.

The effects of the new approach were even more striking in the area of business studies. Here qualifications are, as noted above, taken by many students as a form of extended general education. The curriculum and assessment requirements were completely remodelled so that, instead of learning about the world of business, candidates had to demonstrate their ability to carry out huge numbers of 'core' office tasks. In the most popular such qualification, for example, the new module on finance was rewritten to involve practical demonstration of twelve 'competences':

1 make and record petty cash payments;
2 receive and record payments and issue receipts;
3 prepare for routine banking transactions;
4 make payments to suppliers and others;
5 reconcile incoming invoices for payment;
6 prepare and dispatch quotations, invoices and statements;
7 process expense claims for payments;
8 order office goods and services;
9 process documentation for wages and salaries;
10 process direct payment of wages and salaries;
11 arrange credit transfers;
12 maintain cash book.

This stance has been modified somewhat, in the face of protest about the actual concerns and destinations of candidates; but the general principle remains. All assessment must be of 'competent performance' – the ability actually to apply and use skills and knowledge in authentic situations. As a result, separate tests of maths, communication skills, science and the like are taboo.

The key requirement is that 'evidence of performance is required in respect of *each* element of competence' (NCVQ 1991: 14). In other words, sampling is ruled out. 'Assessment practices such as sampling . . . are all imports from an educational model of assessment which have little place in the assessment of competence'. Similar conclusions tend to follow from any whole-hearted attempt to apply an 'authentic' assessment philosophy, since, if one wants to generalize to applied behaviour, and reach definitive statements about competence and performance, there is always a strong case to be made for direct assessment of any of the outcomes under consideration. However, as other chapters in this book make clear when discussing recent experiences of authentic assessment in English primary schools, the results can easily overwhelm a system.

The emphasis on the real and the authentic also leads NCVQ to emphasize that 'Assessment of performance in the course of normal work offers the most natural form of evidence of competence and has several advantages, both technical and economic' (NCVQ 1991: 14). If 'direct' performance evidence is inadequate, some written or oral 'supplementary questioning' is allowed, checking the relevant skills *in context*. But any such supplementary evidence is second best: to the degree that it is forced upon the teacher or assessor, it should take the form of simulations that are as realistic as possible, since 'the validity of such tests depends on how closely they replicate what is required at work' (NCVQ 1991: 23). Again, there have been widespread attacks on this approach (Hodkinson 1990; Prais 1991): but the top officials of the NCVQ remain unmoved. Vocationally related qualifications, they argue, are about applying knowledge, skills, and so on to real-life problems. If the emphasis on performance assessment is ever allowed to slip, so too will the ultimate value of the whole system.

The effects on classroom practice

The development of this assessment philosophy, in conjunction with the other institutional and funding changes outlined above, has had major effects at classroom level. In describing these, the following section draws on two research projects carried out for the NCVQ and the Department of Employment, which examined the way in which the knowledge 'underpinning' vocational qualifications was being delivered in colleges, and the training needs of staff responsible for NVQ assessment (Wolf 1988; 1992). Three major issues emerged.

First, there has been a huge *increase in the volume of assessment*, and the amount of class time devoted to it. Take, for example, the award in business studies already mentioned above. The finance module which we summarized is one of five which any student must take in the course of a 30-week year. Within each module there are 12 or so practical outcomes ('elements') in which competence must be demonstrated directly. Moreover, how these outcomes are assessed is very tightly constrained. The reforms are assessment-led, not simply in the sense that succeeding in new qualifications has been the way into academic institutions, but also in the way that passing the whole syllabus is embodied in the assessment requirements. Each element in each module is described using a long list of criteria, each of which must, in its turn, be demonstrated by the candidate and assessed by the teacher. (As discussed above, sampling is ruled out.)

Of course, some of the evidence required for different areas can be collected simultaneously: and curriculum materials designed expressly to provide 'assessments' for the new awards have sold well – producing the sort of curriculum packages designed by publishers which are familiar to American educators. However, there are limits to how far this can be done – especially given the modular structure of the courses, and the tendency for different teachers to teach and assess different parts. Many teachers in this sector feel that they are increasingly unable to do any real teaching beyond the narrowest interpretation of the assessment specifications.

In the following quotation from our fieldnotes, a head of business studies summarizes teachers' concerns:

> Real integration is no longer possible. Because the course is unit-based, workshops have been set up to deliver the different elements on a modular basis. This has meant fragmentation of the course and isolation for the staff concerned. Before, with an integrated course, there was potential for creativity and trust in staff judgement. The students are using their brains less and less.

A corollary of the growth in assessment volume is the absence of any hierarchy among the assessment targets. Because everything has to be covered, every outcome is treated as equally important: even though some may be quite trivial, and others concerned with higher-order skills with far more potential for transfer. There is, by design, no distinction made between them, since the essence of the performance-assessment approach adopted is that, if something is specified, it is because it is an essential part of the competence concerned. However, there is potentially a serious danger here, which is that, if time is short – as it invariably is – and resources limited, the temptation is actually to cover a high proportion of trivial targets and 'fudge' on the more difficult ones. There is no incentive to the teacher to do the opposite – and no check on whether this is what has happened.

Second, because of the huge assessment load, and the delegation of assessment to the immediate trainer or teacher, *formative assessment tends to disappear*. The formal philosophy of current practice is that only success is to be emphasized, never failure. Thus, the correct figure of speech is to refer to candidates as being 'ready for assessment'. Ideally, the candidate and teacher or assessor should decide jointly when that time has come, at which point the assessment takes place. It is either successfully accomplished, or the candidate is found to be 'not yet competent' and requiring further practice and reassessment.

It might seem, at first, as though this is an approach which encourages formative assessment. In practice, however, it means that every possibility for 'final assessment' is seized instead. The effort to 'amass evidence' across all assessment targets encourages teachers to take each and every piece of 'successful' performance as evidence that the target in question has been achieved. This has obvious dangers. There will be error variance in any assessment system. However, a system which builds in enormous variation among students and classes with respect to when and how the assessment is carried out will obviously tend to increase such variation. The approach also dissuades teachers from getting involved in formative assessment. Offering informal feedback to students might destroy a perfectly good 'assessment occasion' and the chance of ticking off one of the assessment requirements.

Third, alongside the shift to performance assessment there has been a *breakdown of inter-assessor networks*. This is not itself the result of the shift to authentic assessment, but has happened, unfortunately, at exactly the time when new qualifications and requirements make them more necessary than ever.

In any form of complex judgemental assessment – which includes all the major academic examination systems of Europe, university assessment, and apprenticeship and professional qualifications in most of the world – close contact between assessors is a precondition of both reliable assessment and effective teaching (see, for example, Orr and Nuttall 1983; Wolf 1993). In the UK further education sector, such contacts at present are being undermined rather than strengthened. This is the result of other institutional changes, discussed briefly above, especially the increasing competition between colleges which has followed their independence from LEA control.

The point is a general and important one, nevertheless. Competition between educational institutions is common, especially at the post-compulsory level. Equally, in any form of 'authentic' assessment, assessor networks are indispensable. They become particularly important when new forms of assessment are being introduced, and emphasize the need to consider assessment reform not in isolation but as part of a whole institutional framework.

Critics of authentic assessment tend to focus on issues of reliability; its advocates on the pointlessness of reliable tests with minimal validity, and on the fact that, in the right conditions, high levels of reliability can be reached outside the traditional psychometric framework. The advocates are, of course, correct – high levels of reliability can be reached in, for example, essay-type examinations, as studies of, for example, English A levels, university finals and Civil Service entrance examinations demonstrate (Edgworth 1890; Murphy 1978; 1982) However, it is also evident that these reliability levels are achieved only when the assessors in question are part of a tightly knit group which has a great deal of ongoing, shared experience – not only in teaching but also in the assessment process itself.

The more genuinely 'authentic' the assessment, the more difficult to organize (and expensive) such shared assessment experience becomes. It is none the less vital for all that. Detailed test specifications, from which assessors are expected to construct their own assessments; shared teaching experiences; or the assumption that, in a vocational field, 'experts' will know what the required standard actually is, are demonstrably not enough. The next section of this chapter addresses assessor reliability directly. Here, however, we would emphasize the way in which current assessment requirements, by demanding very large volumes of authentic assessment, make it ever harder and more expensive to create joint assessment networks; and the fact that, because teachers and trainers are in competition with each other for contracts, students, and so on, there is less and less possibility of creating cross-site networks.

Current evidence on reliability

The previous sections of this chapter have raised issues of reliability in a general and theoretical way: and this is largely the level at which the debate in the UK has been taking place. On the one hand, we have had vocal critics of the whole NVQ regime arguing that the inherent unreliability of the approach calls for a return to centrally set paper-based testing (Prais 1991). On the other, the system's designers have argued that, in a system where highly specific assessment criteria are provided and the assessments themselves are authentic examples of the 'competences' in question, reliability ceases to be an issue. Thus Burke and Jessup (1990: 195) argue that:

> Reliability is vital in any norm-referenced system because by definition it is concerned with comparing one individual with another [but in] a criterion-referenced assessment the intention is very different. . . . Once external, explicit criteria have been established . . . [there is] an external reference point for assessment. . . . The essential question of validity centres on comparing the judgements made [by the assessors] . . . with the criteria . . . and not between different assessors or assessments. In these circumstances, reliability is not an issue.

Currently Deputy Director of the NCVQ, Jessup (1991: 192) has gone further and argued that 'If two assessments are both valid they will naturally be comparable and thus reliable but this is incidental'. Too much emphasis on reliability may reduce validity, because one *wants* assessors to call on *different* sets of evidence, and 'It is difficult to see in what sense their judgements might be consistent and reliable in such circumstances'. One wants them to be valid 'instead'.

There is a very peculiar definition of reliability implicit in these arguments. However, this section is concerned less with concepts of reliability than with evidence of how the system is actually working. It draws on two further research studies, both commissioned by the Department of Employment, which looked directly at the reliability of authentic assessment in vocational contexts.

The first of these studies examined the judgements on students' work of trainers and teachers in a wide range of institutions (Wolf and Silver 1986). Subjects were asked to administer a practical assessment designed in line with then-current assessment criteria for the new vocational awards; to do so with students who were 'ready for assessment'; and to judge whether or not the students were 'competent' in the relevant skills. The experiment involved two occupational areas, engineering and business studies. In the former, the assessment involved use of a micrometer and was not enormously different from those then in use for further education awards. In the latter, it was an early example of a very unfamiliar mode, requiring preparation and completion of invoices on the basis of quantities of authentic paperwork.

The results demonstrated enormously variable judgements regarding the level of performance at which a student should be judged 'competent' even though the assessment criteria were apparently highly prescriptive. This was particularly true for the assessors in the business studies area; but even among the engineering group, who had recent experiences with national awards incorporating similar practical tests, we found considerable differences. Some assessors demanded perfect performance (albeit on a fairly simple exercise) if a student was to be deemed 'competent', while others were satisfied with performances which fell far short of this.

The results shed considerable doubt on the notion that clear written 'standards' could ensure acceptable practice on their own. On the contrary, the assessors' behaviour showed a universal tendency to ignore written instructions in favour of their own standards and judgements. However, the assessors in this study were deliberately sampled nationally, and did not form part of an assessor network: and the new qualifications and modes of assessment were extremely unfamiliar. It seemed quite possible that, with familiarity, judgements and understandings would become far more consistent.

The second relevant study was carried out five years later in another area, tourism. It involved instructors who were preparing students – many of them adults – for 'Blue Badge Guide' awards. These are held by top-rank tourist guides who provide in-depth commentaries and information, but who are also expected to display practical skills in delivery, organization of tours, and so on. While the awards are more specifically vocational than most of those delivered by the FE sector, they do combine practical work with a great deal of desk study – history, culture, environment, and so on. The awards are examined on a regional basis, with each region having responsibility for its own tests, but with an active network of external examiners from other regions to ensure consistency, and frequent policy meetings and conferences.

As part of the ongoing drive to reform assessment throughout post-compulsory vocational and professional education, the guide organizations had received some money from the government to help them overhaul their examining system and make their

Table 4.1 Rank correlation matrix for markers' scoring of 'authentic' written assignments (site A)

	1	2	3	4	5	6	7	8
marker 1	1							
marker 2	0.99	1						
marker 3	0.70	0.74	1					
marker 4	0.79	0.81	0.84	1				
marker 5	0.54	0.55	0.78	0.69	1			
marker 6	0.62	0.63	0.85	0.71	0.93	1		
marker 7	0.69	0.73	0.81	0.69	0.75	0.78	1	
marker 8	0.73	0.74	0.79	0.72	0.74	0.76	0.91	1

Source: Clark and Wolf (1991)

assessments more 'authentic' – that is, concerned more with actual delivery of knowledge in an interesting way and less with factual recall. We worked with them to help them develop some more applied and authentic tests, and then looked at how far the examiners concerned actually applied these assessments in a reliable fashion (Clark and Wolf 1991).

The data were collected regionally (because each region's syllabus differs), but for experimental purposes candidates were assessed by far more people than would normally be the case. Normally, assessments would be carried out on the basis of one assessor for the written tests, and two for the practical. For the purposes of the research, all candidates in a region (typically between 20 and 30 a year) were assessed by all the region's qualified examiners. The results are displayed in Tables 4.1–4.3.

Tables 4.1–4.3 present the inter-marker reliabilities for three regions. The results indicate that, even in a situation of established networking and good preparation, inter-marker reliabilities can be very variable on the type of 'authentic' assessments currently being developed in the UK. While some markers show very high levels of agreement, for others rank correlations drop as low as 0.45, 0.23 and even 0.16.

Black *et al.* (1989) documented similar findings for Scottish FE

Table 4.2 Rank correlation matrix for markers (site B) with each other and with candidates' scores on written examination of knowledge recall

	marker 1	marker 2	marker 3	marker 4	exam
marker 1	1				
marker 2	0.45	1			
marker 3	0.61	0.14	1		
marker 4	0.48	0.58	0.80	1	
exam	0.17	0.15	0.23	0.16	1

Source: Clark and Wolf (1991)

Table 4.3 Rank correlation matrix for markers' scoring of 'authentic' written assignments (site C)

	1	2	3	4	5	6	7	8
marker 1	1							
marker 2	0.421	1						
marker 3	0.702	0.727	1					
marker 4	0.636	0.452	0.755	1				
marker 5	0.446	0.982	0.724	0.424	1			
marker 6	0.595	0.566	0.921	0.733	0.561	1		
marker 7	0.634	0.489	0.738	0.929	0.475	0.738	1	
marker 8	0.602	0.5	0.886	0.683	0.509	0.973	0.7	1

Source: Clark and Wolf (1991)

colleges introducing new forms of assessment, and also established that networks of accessors and *not* the apparent specificity of assessment criteria, were the key to increasing consistency. However, the Scottish team has also shown how, over the last few years, increasing competition between colleges has broken down pre-existing networks, and reduced any form of contact and collaboration between assessors in the same field but in different institutions.

Institutional prerequisites for assessment: the prisoners' dilemma

It never makes sense to consider assessment systems detached from their institutional context – but least of all in the case of performance-based or other complex (or 'authentic') assessment approaches. As has been argued above, in order to achieve acceptable levels of reliability – and so, in the long term, credibility – these require frequent contact among assessors, in order to create a 'community of judgement' for which formal instructions and procedures cannot substitute.

These institutional underpinnings are costly. The costs may – indeed, often will – be justified by the advantages of such assessments in terms of feedback into learning and the generalizability of their findings. But the costs are none the less substantial, and the education system concerned must ensure that they are allowed for since quality demands that they be incurred.

Current British reforms have unfortunately combined, at post-compulsory level, an increasing emphasis on performance-based or 'authentic' assessment with other changes which make it increasingly difficult to maintain the underpinning assessor networks – and give institutions powerful short-term incentives not to incur the relevant costs. As noted above, the fact that institutions compete not only for student enrolments but also, directly, for funded 'training contracts', gives them a strong incentive to keep costs down, and to minimize inter-institution cooperation. An additional pressure has recently been introduced in the form of 'payment by results'. Contracts from the Department of Employment provide higher payments for students who complete their courses successfully, and obtain a qualification, than for those who fail. In a system where almost all assessment is carried out by the teachers, this inevitably creates pressures, at the margin, to pass rather than fail students.

Of course, in the long term, a strategy which sacrifices assessment quality, and in which major gaps open up between the rhetoric and the reality of an assessment system, is not sustainable. Among students deciding where, among competing institutions, to enrol, there may be short-term advantages in choosing an institution where standards are low. In the longer term, as this becomes known, the opposite is as likely: supposedly equivalent qualifications are recognized as not equivalent at all, and become worth more or less according to whether they were taken at a 'tough' or an 'easy' college. This is familiar to anyone involved in North American education, but we find examples of the same in, for example, the German apprenticeship system. Here the key point in a young person's life is not the end of apprenticeship, and obtaining the qualification, but the beginning – where that young person gets taken on. However, it has not, until recently, been a feature of British education in the post-compulsory, non-university sector; and it is, of course, the antithesis of the situation which the 'authentic' assessment movement in the UK is attempting to achieve.

Many players in the current British system are, of course, well aware of these issues, and of the danger that the 'product' they are offering will become devalued and lose credibility. They are, however, caught in something of a classic 'prisoners' dilemma' situation. In the long term, it would be better for all of the educational institutions and examining bodies if they expressed their anxieties, confessed where they have been cutting corners, identified the shortfall between the reality and the rhetoric of current performance assessment, and thus forced change on the system. However, no one institution or player feels able to do this. Because they are involved in all-out market competition – at both college (teaching) and certifying level – they feel that, if they speak out, their competitors will simply deny that the problems apply to them at all. Similarly, if they decide to invest large amounts of money in additional quality development, they will simply lose out in bids against other cost-cutters.

In the 'prisoners' dilemma' problem, two prisoners, both involved in the same serious crime, are each offered a reduced sentence in return for evidence against the other prisoner. If *both* keep silent, *neither* can be convicted; and they have, in advance, promised each other to do just that. However, neither trusts the other to keep the promise; and rather than see the other culprit get off easily while they serve a long sentence, they both, ineluctably, arrive at the decision to give evidence against the other. A lack of trust thus produces the worst possible outcome for them, in which both go to prison.

Figure 4.1 shows the situation facing British colleges and examining bodies in standard prisoners' dilemma terms. The bottom right-hand corner shows the current situation, in which they dare not

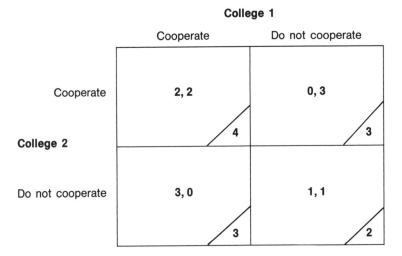

Figure 4.1 Cooperation between colleges in a competitive sector as a case of prisoners' dilemma (numbers represent total 'benefit' of different strategies for each college and (at bottom right of cell) overall)

speak out or cooperate, because they do not trust their competitors. The result is a situation of high costs and anxiety, and lower-quality assessments. We represent the overall 'benefits' to an individual college and its students as having a value of 1 (hence a total of 2 for two colleges in this 'game'). The top left-hand corner shows the benefits if the colleges cooperated, told the truth, rationalised the system and reduced costs – benefits represented as 2 units each for a total of 4. The other two cells represent the situation if one college told the truth and the other did not – a situation where the truth-telling college would lose its reputation and students (value 0) while the other cleaned up (value 3). Fear of this eventuality traps both in the low-value option.

Conclusion

The purpose of this chapter has not been to condemn any form of authentic or performance assessment, or to suggest that it is necessarily doomed to failure. On the contrary, we would fully endorse the criticisms currently being levelled at traditional psycho-metric testing (see, for example, Goldstein 1992).

Nevertheless, it is important to recognize the very real problems which attempts at implementing this form of testing quickly encounter. Advocates need to recognize the costs it involves, and the inherent tendency of these to spiral, as the approach creates ever more assessment demands. It is equally important to grasp that such an approach can only function properly within an appro-priate institutional context and a system of incentives and rewards which recognizes the value of cooperation as well as competition.

Such a system is by no means automatically achieved. On the contrary, it is quite possible for reforms intended to improve the authenticity of classroom assessment to be severely undermined by other institutional changes. In the UK, such changes had, as their origin, concerns with the responsiveness of education to the outside world: concerns which mirror those of the authentic assessment movement. Yet the changes have also, as an unintended conse-quence, destabilized the institutional networks required for a response of high quality.

5

RELIABILITY, VALIDITY AND MANAGEABILITY IN LARGE-SCALE PERFORMANCE ASSESSMENT

Caroline Gipps

Introduction: National Curriculum and assessment

As noted in previous chapters, the Education Reform Act (ERA) of 1988 has brought about wide-ranging changes in education in England and Wales. The Conservative government under Margaret Thatcher intended fundamentally to restructure the education system, claiming that this would improve the quality of education in order to help overcome Britain's economic problems. At the heart of these developments was a concern about educational standards in terms of the range of curriculum experiences offered to pupils in different schools, the rigour of teaching in the basic skills, and low expectations of pupil performance. Both the first and last of these three had been a regularly voiced criticism by the (then) independent Her Majesty's Inspectorate (HMI) in England and Wales.

As outlined in earlier chapters, for each subject the curriculum is enshrined in the law. The National Curriculum is organized around attainment targets (ATs) in each subject, and these attainment targets are articulated at each of the ten levels of the national assessment grading system by a series of criteria or statements of attainment (SOAs) which form the basic structure of a criterion-referenced assessment system. The national assessment programme requires that pupils be assessed against all the ATs by their teachers and on some ATs by external tests (called Standard Assessment Tasks or SATs[1]) at the ages of 7, 11 and 14. At these ages the results are combined and must be reported towards the end of that school year. At 16 the external test is to be the General Certificate of Secondary Education (GCSE) which is currently taken by approximately 85% of the age group.

At the end of Key Stages the pupil's performance is to be reported in terms of levels (including at age 7 separate arithmetic, spelling and reading levels) and comparative information is to be given about all the other pupils of the same age or stage. This comparative information, of course, makes the production of local league tables easy, even at age 7. League tables of school performance are to be published at age 11 and 16. Reporting on performance (Department of Education and Science Circular 7/92) is now structured *specifically* to allow comparative tables of school performance in public examination results at 16 and 18 (which are to be distributed by primary and middle schools to parents of children about to transfer to secondary school and published by the Department for Education in local newspapers). In summer 1993 plans also to publish league tables at ages 7 and 14 were dropped.

While the overall plan for national assessment is the same for all four ages, there are differences in articulation: national assessment at 16 is dominated by the demands of GCSE; the assessments for 11-year-olds are as yet being piloted; the 14-year-old assessments were trialled in 1991, formally piloted in 1992 and then boycotted by the majority of teachers in 1993 when full implementation was attempted. It is the assessment of 7-year-olds which is furthest along the path of development. The detailed account of the national assessment programme which follows is therefore based largely on the developments thus far in the assessment of 7-year-olds. The issues which are raised are, however, relevant to any large-scale, criterion-referenced performance-assessment programme, but particularly with young children.

The assessment of 7-year-olds

During the spring and early summer term of the year in which pupils reach the age of 7 (Year 2) teachers make an assessment of each pupil's level of attainment on levels 1–4 of the scale 1–10 in relation to the ATs of the core subjects. Teachers may make these assessments in any way they wish, but observation, regular informal assessment and keeping examples of work are all encouraged. In the second half of the spring term and the first half of the summer term pupils are given, by their teacher, a series of SATs covering a sample of the core ATs. It should be noted, however, that while these are externally devised tasks, their administration and marking is still done by the pupils' own teachers. This is likely to reduce comparability, as discussed below.

Because of the reliance on teacher assessment, the report of the Task Group on Assessment and Testing (TGAT 1988) suggested a complex process of group moderation through which teachers' assessments could be brought into line around a common standard. The combination of teacher assessment (TA) and SAT results has been a contentious area; the ruling currently is that where an AT is assessed by both TA and SAT and the results differ the SAT result is to be 'preferred'. In future they will be reported separately, which is also likely to privilege the results of the Standard Tasks *de facto*, if not *de jure*. In 1991 and 1992, if the teacher did not agree with the result for an individual pupil she could appeal if the SAT result would alter the overall level for the profile component (a group of ATs).

The proposals for the SATs in the TGAT Report were innovatory and were a conscious attempt to move away from traditional standardized procedures. The report suggested that a mixture of instruments including tests, practical tasks and observations be used in order to minimize curriculum distortion and that a broad range of assessment instruments sampling a broad range of ATs would discourage the narrowing tendency to teach to the test. Thus the TGAT model was one which emphasized a wide range of assessment tasks involving a wide range of response modes, in order to minimize the negative effects normally associated with formal assessment, and a range of assessments in different contexts to ensure content and task validity. Although 'performance assessment' was not a term used widely in the UK in 1987–8, the SATs were clearly performance assessments, using the criteria of authenticity, directness and cognitive complexity (Moss 1992).

Early on in the development of the SATs for Key Stage 1 the requirement was that they should cover as many ATs as possible. This proved unwieldy since there were 32 ATs in the original curriculum structure for the core and the mode of assessment was to be active rather than paper-and-pencil tests of the traditional standardized type (see Torrance 1993b). In the event, the SATs used with 7-year-olds in 1991 were a watered-down version of the TGAT proposals. The style of assessment was, however, active and similar to good infant school practice – for example, the reading task at level 2 involved reading aloud a short passage from a children's book chosen from a list of popular titles, using dice to play maths 'games', using objects to sort, and so on. Despite the reduction in the number of ATs tested from 32 to nine, the Key Stage 1 SAT administration in 1991 took a minimum of 40 hours for a class of 25–30 and was rarely managed without support for the class teacher, since most of the SATs were done with groups of four pupils.

In response to the widespread publicity about the amount of time the 7-year-old SATs were taking, the Prime Minister announced in the summer of 1991 that for 1992 there would be shorter standardized paper-and-pencil tests. (This announcement was made *before* formal evaluations of the SATs were available.) The 1992 SATs contained a reduced number of active tasks, and offered for a number of SATs a 'whole-class' administrative procedure, which in fact few teachers used. The reading SAT remained as a reading-aloud task with the teachers making a running record and in addition an accuracy score. There were also two extra tests: a traditional group reading comprehension test with written response, and a group spelling test. The reading test was optional at level 2 and above and the spelling test was compulsory for level 3 and above. These two scores had to be reported separately alongside the maths 'number' score, as well as the overall levels for English, maths and science.

Current developments

For 1993 there were further changes, with spelling and reading comprehension tests compulsory for all except level 1 as well as the reading and writing Standard Tasks (STs). Different ATs in maths and science are covered each year in addition to 'arithmetic' so that in 1993 7-year-olds were assessed on algebra and physics. The testing package should have taken around 30 hours of classroom time, as it did in 1992. Thus at Key Stage 1 we have a system which is a mix of STs (performance-type assessment), more traditional standardized tests and TA. In the event there was a widespread teacher boycott of the testing in 1993.

At Key Stage 2, age 11, there are group tests (*not* tasks) in English (two hours) Maths (1–1¼ hours) and science (1–1¼ hours). These tests are to be standardized and differentiated – that is, the tests will be at three levels of difficulty covering levels 1–3, 3–5 and 5–6, and pupils must be entered at the appropriate level. As with Key Stage 1 in 1992 and 1993, the 'process' ATs in each subject are not covered by the SAT, but assessed by TA. While this is probably a more satisfactory way of assessing these skills, it does mean that we run the danger of this part of the curriculum becoming downgraded since it is not included in 'high stakes' testing.

Similarly, the trialling of SATs for 14-year-olds which took place in 1991 involved extended tasks taking many hours of classroom time and covering a range of activities and response modes. The Secretary of State for Education deemed this inappropriate and the pilot 'SATs' in 1992 (and the STs designed for 1993) were short written tests done by whole classes at the same time under examination conditions. Practical tests are only to be set where there is no alternative.

Implementing Standard Assessment Tasks

The 1991 SATs for 7-year-olds were by and large performance assessments. For example, multiplication, subtraction and addition were assessed through children throwing dice as in a game and having to add or multiply the numbers thrown on the dice. Floating and sinking in science was assessed through a practical task in which the children were provided with a range of objects and a large tank of water. The children had to predict which objects would float or sink and try and develop a hypothesis. (Since it could take a week or more to assess a whole class of children on this particular task, at one point in the summer term every infant school classroom could be seen to be full of water, waterlogged objects and rotting pieces of fruit – all the children were reported to have enjoyed it!) At level 2 reading was assessed by children reading aloud from a book chosen from a range of good children's story books (the list of 20 story books to be used at this level was published first in a national newspaper, and within a week all the books were out of stock from bookshops); they were assessed by their teachers for fluency as they read and then asked questions when they had finished reading in order to test their comprehension. In addition, there were some paper-and-pencil tasks to be done in maths on an illustrated worksheet and a story to be written in order to assess writing. In the majority of tasks, however, the children did not have to write their answers. Teachers were allowed to help the children produce the written answer, for example in science, and were allowed to make their own judgements about whether the child understood or was able to do the task in hand. Bilingual children were allowed to have an interpreter for the maths and the science tasks. Listening and speaking was not assessed by a SAT: early on in the development process it was decided that this was better assessed by teachers' own judgement.

Manageability

What did this mean for schools and teachers? In our evaluation study, also discussed in Chapter 3, we worked intensively with teachers in 32 schools in four different local education authorities (LEAs). We found that due to the style of assessment, with children having to be assessed individually or in small groups, considerable changes were required to school organization in order to support the class teachers and to cater for the children who were not being assessed (Gipps *et al.* 1992). Schools where team teaching took place and schools where classes were not composed entirely of 7-year-old pupils generally found this task easier. Schools where there were classes made up entirely of 7-year-old pupils however had the most reorganization to effect. Considerable changes were made in some schools to support the administration of the testing. This often had a knock-on effect on other staff and where disruption was widespread – for example, removal of all in-class support from other classes to the Year 2 class, or removal of Year 2 teachers from all playground and other duties – contributed to stress within the school as a whole. However, collegial support for Year 2 teachers was the rule rather than the exception: colleagues offered high levels of support in order to protect the Year 2 teachers from what was seen as an appallingly difficult, stressful and time-consuming activity rather than to perform the assessments particularly well or quickly. In half of our schools the head teachers themselves were actively involved in doing the SATs or support activities and welcomed the opportunity to spend time with the children. Stress was due not only to the added pressure of having to do the assessment but also to the enormously high level of publicity that the assessments received, hitherto unheard of at primary level, and to many teachers' anxiety about formally assessing children as young as this with assessments which they felt could be used for labelling children. The culture of UK primary teachers maintains that assessment of young children should be only for diagnostic purposes, that labelling, and indeed sorting children according to ability or achievement, is improper, particularly at an age as young as 7 where many children will only have had five full terms of schooling. Teachers are all too well aware of the effect of different lengths of time in school due to birth date, different types of pre-school provision, and different family and social backgrounds (especially for ethnic minority children from non-English speaking homes) on children's performance. Thus stress was due to a range of factors related to: a major innovation, the fact of assessment, and the high profile of the activity. An anxiety that we anticipated as researchers was that because of the complexity of the assessment programme and the stress that it caused, it would succeed in turning teachers off assessment in general; this was a very real danger.

The 1992 exercise was managed with less stress, partly because it was the second time around and schools knew what to expect, partly because two long practical tasks were dropped. However, the testing still took a considerable amount of time and the administration was by no means standardized so that reliability and manageability were again major issues.

Assessing a class of 25–30 children took 40–45 hours of direct teacher time in 1991, 24 hours plus the time for the reading assessments in 1992 (National Foundation for Educational Research/

Bishop Grossteste College (NFER/BGC 1992)), and arrangements had to be made for other children while individuals or small groups were being tested by the teacher. Whether this seems manageable depends partly on the perceived value of the assessments.

Reliability

The literature on performance assessment tends to down play issues of reliability (Linn *et al.* 1991; Moss 1992). This is because in the main the use of performance assessment is part of a move away from highly standardized procedures. However, since the major function of the national assessment programme of England and Wales has in the event proved to be accountability and comparability, we cannot avoid questions over reliability. I use the term 'reliability' here in relation to consistency as a basis for comparability; issues of consistent and comparable administration, comparability of the task, and comparability of assessment of performance (among raters) are the focus, rather than technical test-retest or split-half measures of reliability (see also Wiliam 1992).

The administration of SATs is quite different from that of tests: in the SATs the most important consideration is that pupils should understand what is expected of them. Thus there was no restriction on what was said, or on the use of the skills of another adult who is normally present in the classroom. There was no restriction on non-linguistic methods of presentation, there was no limit on pupils working in whatever language or combination of languages they normally used in mathematics or science. However, pupils are not allowed to explain tasks to each other nor may children whose mother tongue is not English have the English tasks explained to them in their mother tongue. While the emphasis on understanding the task is, of course, entirely appropriate for assessing very young children, the lack of standardized introduction for the assessment tasks meant that, as we observed, there was great variation in administration, not only across teachers but also *between administrations by the same teacher*. (See also James and Conner 1993; and Chapter 1 in this volume.)

Other aspects which contributed to variability were: the choice of group for small-group testing; choice of objects, for example for the sorting or floating tasks; and in 1992 choice of worksheet or practical task. The make-up of a small group for an assessment task can have an effect on the performance of individuals within it, and teachers sometimes consciously chose to put shy children into groups which they felt would allow them to perform at their best. In fact we know rather little about the dynamics of small-group assessment but we must assume that they can affect performance. In addition, teachers were allowed to choose the sets of objects for the sorting task, for example, and we observed children in some classrooms sorting sets which appeared to be much easier to classify and sort than in other classrooms, with obvious effects on comparability of performance. Allowing teachers to choose the objects was no doubt meant to reduce the test development load and to provide objects with which the children were familiar, but detailed guidelines and/or lists of objects to be used would have helped to reduce the variability.

Performance assessments cannot be done in large groups with very young children; in order to deal with the manageability issue the assessments for 1992 were less time-consuming and less performance-based so that they could be given to whole classes of children or small groups (in fact, most teachers chose *not* to use the whole-class format). But offering the assessment as a whole-class or a small-group activity in itself is likely to alter the difficulty of the task. Furthermore, sometimes the task could be offered as a practical task *or* done using a worksheet; this, of course, changes the nature of the task and is an unnecessary additional cause of variability. Studies by Shavelson *et al.* (1992) and Koretz *et al.* (1991) suggest that testing similar content in different assessment modes is unlikely to produce similar results; both papers indicate that the standardized (multiple-choice) tests are probably assessing different aspects of the subject than are the performance-based assessments.

Finally, the SOAs are not always sufficiently clear to allow teachers to make unambiguous judgements about performance; the criteria in this criterion-referenced assessment system were not specific enough for assessment purposes. In some schools, which we describe as analytic, teachers discussed criteria and standards of performance among themselves, and in these schools it is likely that assessments were more standardized and more comparable across classes than in other schools (Gipps 1992), a finding supported by the official evaluation in 1992 (NFER/BGC 1992). In the schools where discussion did take place it was partly because of the woolliness of the assessment criteria that these discussions were started.

Owing to the inadequacy of the SOAs there has been some concern over teacher judgements in the SATs and TA. The technical evaluations carried out in 1991 indicate that SOAs were indeed interpreted differently by different teachers (NFER/BGC 1991) and that assessments made of the same attainment target by TA, SAT and an alternative test had unacceptable levels of variation (Shorrocks *et al.* 1992; Harlen 1993). The 1992 evaluation (NFER/BGC 1992) found that the match between TA levels and SAT levels was significantly greater in the second year of the assessment. A range of factors could be causing this, one at least being an artefact of the system rather than necessarily being due to teachers' changing assessment skills. In 1992 teachers did *not* have to commit themselves to their TA levels until *after* the SATs were done; it is possible then that the teachers' own assessments were affected by the SAT results; it is also possible that some teachers did not make a separate TA but simply used the SAT result where an attainment target was assessed by both.

The evidence on inter-rater reliability in National Curriculum assessment is limited in the UK, other than the comparison of TA and SAT level, which is of dubious value. Furthermore, the supervising body, the School Examinations and Assessment Council (SEAC), has admitted that there were good reasons for TA and SAT results *not* to align. TA, although less standardized, covers a wider range of attainments over a longer period of time. Thus it may be less accurate than SAT assessment but is more thorough and offers a better description of overall attainment: 'The two forms of assessment should not therefore be regarded as identical' (SEAC 1991: 34). The determination of mastery was also an issue in 1991 and 1992: for the SATs all but one SOA had to be achieved to gain a particular level while in TA there was no such rule, and we do not know how teachers made their mastery decisions.

There is some evidence from the development of performance-based maths tasks for Key Stage 3 that inter-rater reliability was higher on these than on the written tests (Brown 1992). This rather tentative finding is supported by the work of Shavelson *et al.* (1992) which found that when observers are trained and scoring rubrics provided, inter-rater reliability for performance-based tasks is high.

By contrast, the standardized paper-and-pencil tests of reading comprehension and spelling that were introduced into the 1992 Key Stage 1 national assessment in order to enhance 'objectivity' were not scored particularly reliably. When booklets were remarked in the reading test the original mark and the remark corresponded exactly in only 55% of cases and 72% of cases for the spelling test (NFER/BGC 1992).

Evidence on inter-rater reliability of the SATs is therefore patchy, but there is some evidence (James and Conner 1993; NFER/BGC 1992) which our case studies would support that teachers in schools who have, or make, the opportunity to discuss standards of performance are developing common standards for assessment. As James and Conner (1993) point out, the SEAC Handbook for moderators emphasized consistency of approach (to conducting the assessments) *and* consistency of standards (inter-rater reliability) which were to be achieved in 1991 and 1992 through the moderation process. Certainly it would seem that the process of group moderation – called 'social moderation' by Linn (1992) – in which groups of teachers, with or without a 'moderator', or external expert, come together and discuss pieces of work or what counts as performance, greatly aids comparability, and other chapters in this book report such evidence and discuss the process in more detail. In some of our schools the process was going on but it needs to be supported and routinized if it is to have any serious impact on variability/standardization.

From 1993, however, the process came to be called 'auditing', the term moderation having been dropped (Department for Education 1992). The key difference is that rather than offering a system which supports moderation of the process and procedure of the assessments, evidence will be required that results conform to national standards: head teachers will have to ensure that teachers become familiar with national standards and keep evidence of assessment and records for audit when required. Concern about national levels of consistency has thus been acknowledged by the government, but the issue of putting in place a significant process of moderation has been side-stepped.

Validity

The style of the SAT was premised on an attempt to enhance the validity of the task. I am here referring to the content and construct aspects of validity (Nuttall 1987; Messick 1989). I shall deal with consequential validity later in this chapter. As Messick (1989), Linn *et al.* (1991) and Moss (1992) point out, consideration of social consequences of test use is critical in any consideration of validity. In the UK this latter aspect of validity has received relatively little attention, which is unfortunate to say the least, given the accountability uses to which the results are put at the school and LEA level, and the likely uses (selection, grouping) at the individual level.

Descriptions already given of the SATs indicate their nature and likely content and construct validity. The case-study work of James and Conner (1993) carried out in four LEAs suggests, however, that according to teachers a number of the assessments did not validly represent either the content or the construct being assessed – for example, in relation to the writing task where use of full stops and capital letters was important but no judgement was required of the quality of ideas expressed in the writing. This is an issue for the test developers, as the 1992 evaluation recognized (NFER/BGC 1992). This reports some criticism of the quality of the pupil materials and notes that in moving away from practical tasks to paper-and-pencil tasks they need to take 'even greater care in ensuring that pupil materials are of high quality' (NFER/BGC 1992: 158). The authors also report that many teachers who did not use these materials but stayed with a practical approach did so because they were concerned about the validity of the tasks. This in itself suggests an enormous increase in teachers' understanding of assessment issues (cf. Gipps *et al.* 1983).

In attempting to enhance validity through the use of performance-based SATs, however, reliability was often compromised. The reading assessment offers a good example of the tension between reliability and validity which ensued. The reading assessment for level 2 (the expected level of performance for most 7-year-olds) involved children reading aloud from real books and then being asked questions about the content and future events. It was high on content, even construct, validity in that it matches what we think of as real reading for average 7-year-olds. However, part of the attempt to enhance validity was a very cause of the unreliability: there was a choice allowed from a range of 20 books and it was not uncommon for children to be reading from a book which they, it turned out, knew well. Thus obviously for some children the task was much easier since they already knew the story and had practised the reading. Ultimately this also begs questions of validity since in extreme cases the test may only have been testing recall of previously rehearsed knowledge rather than reading comprehension.

Another aspect which enhances validity is that the teacher makes informal observational assessments of the child's fluency and other skills which relate to the SOAs for reading. However, these factors limit the reliability of the assessment because given the choice of texts we cannot assume that the task is comparable, or of comparable difficulty, for all the children, and given the reliance on judgemental factors in the assessment we cannot be sure that all teachers are assessing children at the same level in the same way. These factors tend to limit the comparability of the assessment. Thus we have an assessment that is more valid and less reliable, while a standardized reading test would be more reliable and less valid. The problem lies in getting the most appropriate balance between these two requirements.

In discussing consequential validity the use of National Curriculum assessment results has to be considered at a number of levels. At the level of the individual child we know that the close observation of children's performance on a range of tasks in English, maths and science against a set of (not always clear) criteria has been a rewarding and illuminating activity for many teachers. Despite early claims that the assessments told them nothing new, which our research contradicted (Gipps *et al.* 1992), we have evidence that by late 1992 over half our head teachers believed they could see the beneficial effects of this close observation and detailed assessment on teachers' practice. They felt that testing alone had not been of particular value, but the close observation of children against the detailed curriculum statements had focused teachers' attention on the curriculum, improved their understandings of what children could do and raised expectations. Furthermore, the process of moderation had forced teachers to interact, negotiate meaning for SOAs, standardize judgements about individual children and discuss 'levelness' (McCallum *et al.*

1993). We were also able to document some changes in teaching practice (Gipps *et al.* 1992) which resulted in both an emphasis on the basics of spelling, punctuation and mental arithmetic, and a broadening of teaching to include more practical maths and science work. For some teachers, too, it brought the introduction of group and independent work (Gipps 1992). (It should be said, however, that the majority of infant school teachers already use group and independent work.) Thus, at this level we can see some consequences of the assessment which broadened rather than narrowed teachers' practice.

At the school level, results will be used to put schools into rank-ordered league tables, to encourage schools to compete in the marketplace with the parent as consumer selecting schools, so the rhetoric goes, on the basis of academic excellence. At both a moral and technical level one can critique this approach: encouraging schools to be compared on the basis of academic performance alone downgrades the other important tasks which schools, particularly primary schools, are trying to accomplish and inevitably advantages schools with socially and economically privileged intakes. At a technical level it should be clear from what has been said about reliability that given the undependable nature of results the data are simply not robust enough to be used for this purpose.

The same has to be said about the LEA league tables: despite evidence that the 1991 national assessment results for Key Stage 1 were undependable, the publication of the league table went ahead. The LEA at the bottom was pilloried in the press (*Times Educational Supplement* 1993) although two reasons are apparent for its low performance: large numbers of disadvantaged families and children whose first language is not English, and guidance that was given to the teachers to be as realistic as possible in their assessments (at the time it was believed that the 1991 results would not be reported – the LEA's advice might have been different had it been known they would be published, particularly in this form).

At national level, the government has been able to show that standards have risen since the percentage of the 7-year-old population reaching higher levels has risen in reading, spelling and maths (DFE 21/12/92 'Seven Year Olds Results Show Improving Standards'). Of course, one is left wondering what such a 'rise in standards' means or is worth. Given the changes from 1991 to 1992 and the undependability of results we would be inclined to say that such changes in patterns of performance should be treated with extreme caution.

Conclusion

It is clear that the SAT as originally conceived is simply not appropriate for assessing literally hundreds of assessment points; it becomes too time-consuming for testing whole age groups of pupils, particularly at a certain point in time. For what is essentially survey testing, something quicker and more reliable is needed. The SAT model, on the other hand, is ideal to support individual, formative and diagnostic assessment by teachers for their own purposes. Continuous assessment by teachers can be summed up at the end of Key Stages to give summative information. Politicians, however, tend to take the view that summative assessment, particularly if it is also to be used for evaluative purposes or for certification and selection, must be taken out of the hands of teachers. Thus teacher assessment is not to be used on its own at the end of Key Stages because it is likely to be unreliable and/or biased. So goes the argument. It is, of course, true that teachers do need some form of referencing if their standards are to be nationally comparable, which fairness and equity demand. For public exams at 16 and 18, external markers and moderation processes have been developed to deal with this issue and it is widely accepted (though not necessarily on a particularly good basis) that this produces reliable judgements.

However, an assessment system which relied on widespread moderation and extended marking when applied to four age groups simultaneously would clearly be unmanageable. Fitness for purpose is an issue which was never properly addressed. For those who are interested in 'standards' and whether they are rising or falling, the national assessment programme will not actually be very useful. It will only give us gross indications of performance – the percentage of children at level 1, 2 or 3. The levels are supposed to cover two years' worth of progress so any changes in standards would have to be pretty big to be noticed. If there is limited comparability we cannot place much weight on the results at a national level for accountability and comparison purposes. For monitoring and checking on standards we need to use a different style of assessment, which requires: precise measures in order to show the fairly small shifts in performance that there are only ever likely to be (difficult); tests which do not date (even more difficult); fully standardized procedures (not particularly suitable for 7-year-olds) or widespread moderation of less standardized tasks (time-consuming and expensive). But one does not need to test every child: a light (or partial) sample is quite adequate (see Harlen *et al.* 1992), as is the case with the American National Assessment of Educational Performance (NAEP).

The final straw was the complexity of the curriculum structure: this resulted in an enormous number of SOAs which became the assessment criteria in the criterion-referenced assessment system. Requiring teachers to assess all children on every criterion and to report this four times during their school career is difficult enough, but to link this with external, performance-type assessment of all children on a high proportion of these criteria at a particular point in the school year is clearly too daunting and time-consuming a task. The government's solution, to return to narrow, highly standardized tests (at age 11 and 14) and to reduce the curriculum framework so that there are fewer, more general, assessment criteria, is disappointing. It risks all the problems of teaching to the test which were raised when national assessment was first mooted (see, for example, Torrance 1988) and indicates how little cognizance the government takes of the educational assessment community.

More general lessons

As a number of writers have observed (among them Mehrens 1992; Linn 1993) there are problems with using performance assessments for accountability purposes. These problems hinge essentially around issues of manageability, reliability and validity.

The issue that we in the UK have to address is how to achieve acceptable levels of comparability without compromising validity while keeping the assessment programme manageable. Given the uses to which national assessment results in the UK are put, standardization is still privileged because of the need for comparability. As Moss (1992: 251) puts it, no one has yet suggested an alternative means of warranting assessment-based conclusions: 'And so standardised assessment continues to be privileged by commonly accepted validity criteria'. Or as Linn *et al.* (1991) have it: 'if great weight is attached to the traditional criteria of efficiency, reliability and comparability of assessments from year to year, the more complex and time-consuming performance-based measures will compare unfavourably with traditional standardised tests'.

I believe, furthermore, that there are very specific issues related to the age of the children being assessed which mean that they require a different format for an assessment programme. For example, our teachers commonly tried to get the best performance out of the children: by reassuring them, helping them, offering preparation and emotional support and sometimes even a second chance. This is one of the criteria for educational assessment (Wood 1986) and definitely runs counter to the notion of assessment as examination or hurdle. This, we felt, was not due to teachers' particular models of assessment but rather to their view of what is appropriate for children of this age. Teachers were concerned about 'failure' and 'labelling' for such young children and there was some tension between offering children the chance to try the next advanced level in the assessment programme or, indeed, to keep plugging away at a particular assessment task, and the need to prevent the children experiencing failure. Our teachers also went to enormous lengths to hide the fact that this was testing; despite the stress and anxiety reported by teachers, there was very little of this observed when the children were being assessed. The children were generally unaware of the purpose and importance of the tasks that they were engaged in. This was because the teachers were at great pains to ensure that they were protected from what was going on. Very few children were seen to be upset by the activities; some were bored, but it was much more common that children enjoyed them.

It also seems to be the case that when teachers of young children assess those children, either individually or in small groups, it is almost inevitable that they will vary the way in which they introduce the task, whether they have highly specific instructions or not; this is because what the teacher sees is not a testing situation but individual children whom she knows well and who need to have things explained to them in different ways, or presented in different ways, because of the children's own backgrounds, abilities and immediate past history. If this is the case then it will not be possible (and, one might say, not desirable) to have standardized performance assessments with young children.

A general problem with performance assessments, if they are to be used for anything other than instructional purposes, is the limited sampling from a domain and the difficulty then of generalizing from the performance to the whole domain. This is a particular worry since we know that performance on this type of activity is highly task-specific (Shavelson *et al.* 1992; Linn 1993). In the learning of some skills, such as a second language (Swain 1990), variation in performance may be part of the learning process, in which case high internal consistency is not an appropriate criterion to use in seeking a sound assessment.

Linn (1993) argues that to overcome this problem we should increase the number of tasks and ensure comprehensive coverage of the domain in order to improve generalizability. Shavelson *et al.* (1992) suggests the use of a range of tasks and types of assessment activity together with a re-emphasis on assessment for professional purposes rather than for accountability or school reform. Swain (1990: 411) argues that, in relation to second language measures, we need to rethink the whole concept of accuracy and consistency: 'Perhaps we may have to begin a search for "meaningful quality criteria" for the inclusion of test items rather than rely on a measure of internal consistency'. Moss (1992), too, calls for the development of alternative models for warranting validity conclusions (see also Gipps 1994, for a reconceptualization of reliability and validity within educational assessment). Increasing the number of tasks to aid generalizability will, of course, increase the already considerable amount of time taken to carry out the assessments. Linn argues that this can be justified on the grounds that the assessment task itself is a useful part of instruction. But increasing the assessment load, without carrying the politicians' or the public's understanding of what these assessments are for, or are trying to do, will cause problems with public acceptability (Mehrens 1992) as the UK story clearly shows.

Moderation is a key element of performance assessment, not only in terms of improving inter-rater reliability, but also to moderate the *process* of assessment. If we wish to be able to 'warrant assessment-based conclusions' without returning to or resorting to highly standardized procedures, with all that this implies for poor validity, then we must ensure that teachers have common understandings of the criterion performance and the circumstances and contexts which elicit best performance. This suggests that we move towards a performance model (see Fredericksen and Collins 1989) rather than a sampling model, that is to say, concern is with the quality of the performance and fairness in scoring rather than with replicability and generalization.

The disadvantage of group moderation is that it is time-consuming, and this may then be seen to add to any unmanageability. Its great advantage, on the other hand, lies in its effect on teachers' practice. In the UK, and to a certain extent in the Vermont study (Koretz *et al.* 1992), it has been found that where teachers come together to discuss performance standards or criteria it becomes a process of teacher development with positive washback on teaching (see Torrance 1986b; and Chapter 6 in this volume). It seems that coming together to discuss performance or scoring is less personally and professionally threatening than discussing, for example, pedagogy. But discussion of assessment does not end there: issues of production of work follow on and this broadens the scope of discussion and impacts on teaching.

Being realistic, I believe that large-scale performance assessment *can* only cover a limited range of activities, particularly with younger children, because they are by nature time-consuming and may need to be carried out individually or in small groups. In the UK programme this should not be a problem because we have the requirement for TA as well. In other words, what we would be looking for in a high-quality assessment programme is a combination of high-quality, time-consuming performance assessment which covers a changing, smaller number of skills complemented by TA of a much wider range of skills. The advantage of the high-quality performance assessment here is that over the years it can come to support and moderate the teacher's own assessment practice. Such a combination of TA and performance assessment can manageably cover the full range of the curriculum, giving due weight to process and higher-order skills and thus support teaching. How we reach acceptable levels of reliability, if the assessment programme has a prime accountability purpose, is, however, still not clear.

Note

1 SATs are now called Standard Tasks at age 7, and Standard Tasks or Tests at ages 11 and 14.

6

DEVELOPING A COLLABORATIVE APPROACH TO MODERATION

Hilary Radnor and Ken Shaw

Introduction

Moderation is the review and social ratification of teachers' assessments, that is, their judgements of the value of pupils' work. Moderation understood as review is essential to monitor the quality of assessment and to ensure that it is fair, to see that procedures are adhered to, and to check on interpretations – that is, how criteria have been applied to cases. The Moderation and Assessment Project, South West (MAPSW) was funded by the Manpower Services Commission, a UK government agency, to support development of moderation practices in secondary education courses that contained a significant element of practical coursework. Such courses grew out of the expansion of the Technical and Vocational Education Initiative (TVEI) launched by the UK government in 1983.

One aspect of the TVEI was designed to increase the number of courses for 14–16-year-olds that more directly related to the world of work – for example, information technology, business studies and design and technology. Since most children sit the General Certificate of Secondary Education (GCSE) at the age of 16 in

England and Wales, it was considered important that these new courses received national accreditation through the examination boards and within the overall context of GCSE.

The new courses involved a high degree of practical and experiential learning. The evolving theory and pedagogy of TVEI considered 'process' to be as important as product. This led to the questioning of pencil-and-paper terminal examinations as a valid form of assessment for these courses. The examination boards responded by accepting the participation of teachers in the assessment of pupils' work for certification and by appointing moderators to monitor and maintain standards. Given their previous experience and general philosophy, the examination boards were not able to offer training other than of a procedural kind to the moderators, who, therefore, had to discover and negotiate their new role with each other and with teachers.

A previous study funded by one of the boards (the Southern Region Examination Board) conducted by Harry Torrance from 1982 to 1984 investigated the complexity and variety of practice across different subjects in six schools in four local education authorities (LEAs) in the South of England. Torrance (1986a: 49) states:

> Probably the most important point to emerge from the study as a whole is that 'school-based assessment' cannot be treated as a simple coherent entity. Judgements about its worth, its effectiveness and its potential must take into account the different ways in which both examiners and teachers construe and conduct teacher assessment.

The differing views expressed by teachers of the relationship of teachers to the examination boards, the purpose and principles of assessment of pupils' work and the role of the examiners moderating that work across different schools highlighted the lack of a consensual approach and led to concern about the varied and generally uneasy relationships between moderators and teachers. The TVEI coordinators in the South West Region of England decided to tackle the issue. The result was the setting up of the MAPSW. The TVEI coordinators in the seven South West of England education authorities agreed to fund jointly one named person in each authority (to be designated as Assessment Development Officer (ADO)) to conduct research and train together to develop moderation models and skills. Support in directing and evaluating the project was sought from the School of Education, University of Exeter. This resulted in Dr Hilary Radnor directing the project and Dr Ken Shaw evaluating it.

In summary, the MAPSW project was a sustained attempt over a period of three years to identify, clarify, test in the field, reflect upon and express coherently the evolving practice of assessment and moderation as it has been experienced and understood by the ADOs. The outcome of this work is the model of moderation presented in this chapter.

The development of school-based examining

Pressure has been developing for some years now in the UK to increase the integration of assessment more fully with teaching (see Murphy and Torrance 1988, for a review of recent UK developments). A key document in this respect is the report of the Task Group on Assessment and Testing (TGAT 1988) which opens with the contention that assessment of pupils' achievements 'lies at the heart of promoting children's learning' (para. 3).

Secondly, the cumulative effect of the TVEI and the GCSE (first examined in 1988) was to press schools to endeavour to develop new skills, capacities and understandings in pupils – for example, problem-solving, gathering and analysing data, how to apply and use knowledge rather than remember it and how to exploit experiential learning opportunities. Assessing these learning objectives involves the design of relevant tasks in the form of projects and investigations, for example, which enable pupils to show strengths other than those that can be shown in terminal examinations. For obvious reasons of cost and logistics, teachers are in the best position to observe pupils at work over a period of time. Assessment of pupils' work in these conditions is not straightforward, and there is a demand that teachers' judgements be monitored and validated.

Thirdly, as Torrance (1989) stressed in a later article, the issue of reliability as well as validity led examination boards to become interested in considering a broader sample of pupils' work than could be provided by the one-off, sit-down terminal test or examination. Only teachers could provide it, yet since the late 1980s we have been in a period of distrust of teachers, of concern for accountability and interest in using the results of testing and examining as performance indicators for judging the success of schools.

The processes and procedures of moderating teacher assessments of coursework and practical work actually have quite a long practical pedigree in the UK, but studies of moderation are not common. Schools Council Bulletin 37 (1977) noted that the introduction of the Certificate of Secondary Education (CSE) in 1963 (one of the forerunners of GCSE) meant that teachers 'have begun to play a significant part in the assessment of their own pupils' work in the context of the public examination'. Schools Council Bulletin No. 37 saw teachers as capable of complementing the work of external examiners, offsetting the unreliability of the one-off examination. Moderation, then, served to establish standards among differing schools. Alternatively, teachers could be sole assessors of what is inaccessible to the external examination: oral work, fieldwork, practical music, drama, science or craft.

The experience of MAPSW has been that these processes of moderation are problematic not only in technical and logistic terms, but also because they raise issues of power-sharing between teachers and examination board officials. They also raise questions of dignity, and professional self-respect, of involvement in decision-making, of skill and training, of the confidence teachers have in their own judgement, and of the lack of agreed and tested principles and working models, as opposed to generalized, well-intentioned official statements.

The majority of published material dealing specifically with moderation (Secondary Examinations Council 1985; 1986; 1988; Bennetts 1986; Kempa 1986; Good and Cresswell 1988; School Examination and Assessment Council 1991a) does not draw upon detailed fieldwork with teachers and schools. The MAPSW project was designed to draw from such fieldwork in order to develop an assessment and moderation package that was, as far as possible, straightforward, coherent and sensitive to the needs of both learners and teachers, linking notions of public credibility with teacher-based assessment and moderation practices.

MAPSW project: method and procedure

The ADOs had two two-day residential 'conferences' a year, over three years. For each conference, the group met from 10.00 a.m. on day 1 until 4.00 p.m. on day 2, residing in hotels in the different counties.

The professional development model favoured by the tutor/director was to enable the ADOs to link the conferences together by engaging in research activities between the conferences. The purpose of this was to develop knowledge and understanding in the area of assessment/moderation. Evidence was collected in the field and ideas generated at the conferences. The ADOs also tested out their deliberations and analysis subsequently with colleagues in their own county. These research strategies reinforced the shared collaborative activities that took place at the conferences themselves. Each conference was structured so that, by the end of the conference each ADO had formulated an action plan of activities to undertake between conferences. These developed out of the end-point of the conference itself. Each conference had a particular focus.

The first conference (September 1988) mapped out the future programme for the project, the key intention of which was to establish a teacher-moderation model in the schools and colleges with emphasis on the 14–19 age range. The focus was put as a research question: what does the project want from a teacher-moderation model for school/college-based work? At the second conference (January 1989) three case studies were presented of teachers engaged in assessment and moderation of coursework. The main issues that emerged out of the case studies were noted and categorized into themes. These formed the basis of areas of investigation and enquiry for the first round of ADO research projects in the field.

The third conference (June 1989) generated a set of assessment and moderation principles based on the empirical evidence presented both by the projects and also by the ADOs' own developing experience. The next stage was to undertake empirical work to see if the principles could be grounded in practice. The ADOs agreed to devise projects to 'test out' principles and to give feedback to a later conference. Ownership, responsibility and partnership were issues that had to be tackled together with the relationship of the teachers to the examining boards and the boards to the public. The MAPSW principles seek partnership between examining agencies and teachers in teacher-assessed coursework. There is acceptance of the need for teachers to take responsibility for a rigorous self-regulating system that gives credibility to the idea of having ownership of assessment as well as of teaching processes.

The fourth conference (November 1989) came at the time when Standard Assessment Tasks (SATs, National Curriculum assessment) were being trialled and there was much debate about National Vocational Qualifications (vocational assessment). This conference became an updated 'teach-in' of national assessment practices concentrating on issues such as criteria-referenced assessment and teachers' ability to assess with validity and reliability. A further round of field projects was negotiated. The fifth conference (June 1990) centred around the findings of these. The ADOs retained a belief in the principles as a foundation for good practice as strongly after the field testing as before. Some even used them as a basis for evaluation – that is, taking the principles and seeing how the practice matched up to them. Where there were incongruities, they sought out why. They wanted to know if the principles were workable in practice and whether the assessment or moderation arrangements already in operation were deficient in some way and could be improved by following MAPSW developments. Others were engaged in moderation and/or assessment activities and, having been part of the process, then reflected on the principles to help them to evaluate the practices in which they were engaged. The overall outcome was clearly that the principles were perceived to be a sound basis from which to proceed and out of which it was possible to develop a moderation model. A number of issues emerged and the conference went a long way towards developing what was considered to be an appropriate model. The initial research question, concerning what the project wants from a teacher-moderation model for school/college-based work, was virtually answered.

The purpose of the project was to offer a way forward, to give a lead to changes in moderation practice. This chapter now describes the model, which we term the *reconciliation model*. It is introduced by stating the philosophy underlying the model, arrived at through the collaborative work of the ADOs, the project director and the evaluator, and agreed by all. The model is then described and the chapter concludes with a short case study to show how the reconciliation model works in practice.

The philosophy underlying the model

First, the model stresses wholeness/integration of the process of planning, teaching and assessment, as opposed to bolt-on, fragmentation, *ex post facto* moderation. The 'old' assessment model was largely a descendant of the traditional interest of the boards in certificating attainment on the basis of terminal material produced by students under examination conditions. It tended to be distant, external, authoritative, with the moderator as a board appointee, a powerful outsider in the role of arbiter of assessment. The principles of interpretation and ideas about standards were frequently explicit, or embodied in general official reports some time after the moderation, and only diffused back through the teachers to the pupils as a result of long experience of playing the examination game, rather than as feedback to assist the teaching/learning directly. The rapid developments that have been described in the introduction – TVEI, GCSE and so on – have shown the limitations of this approach: a 'new' assessment model is rapidly developing alongside the old, which sees the process of conceiving, planning and delivering the course, and the assessment, moderation and feedback of information as an integrated whole, and integral to the intention to use assessment and moderation to improve teaching and learning.

Second, assessment and moderation should be based in the institutions and made part of teachers' and others' professionalism through the accreditation of LEAs, consortia of institutions or individual institutions. The old moderation was seen generally as an event, where one person, using his or her own experience, standing and intuitive skills in evaluating students' work, acted as the ratifier and carrier of common standards among institutions. The task was seen essentially as 'checking', or even remarking, a sample of the submitted work, adjusting the marks or ranges to the satisfaction of the boards. The new moderation sees the activity as a partnership carrying out a process of ratifying the values assigned to students' work during the process of the learning as well as terminally. It is a process of discussion and negotiation resulting in the creation of a socially constructed consensus among the participants, teachers, boards and LEAs, in which the public is (as in legal contracts) a silent interested party to which all are accountable.

Third, the model accepts the importance of positive assessment based on appraisal of what students know, understand and can do. For validity, a larger sample than that traditionally associated with terminal examination is required; process as well as end-products of learning come under review. The problem of monitoring active learning and the results of students' opportunities for experiential learning are confronted.

Fourth, the model accepts the need for social ratification by outside bodies of the values assigned by the teacher assessors to the pupils' work, and therefore the need for external moderators and certification by the boards. Just as an appropriate curriculum is an entitlement of students, so is good assessment. The necessary acquisition of assessment and moderation skills and knowledge is a professional obligation on all participants.

Fifth, the model takes a particular view of the nature of knowledge and learning. A purely cognitive grasp of information and principles is not the only form that certifiable attainment takes. The outcomes of learning extend beyond retained and well-patterned information to include the ability to use and apply the information effectively, to be able to extend it independently and to have insight and understanding into how the information is put to use to assist in identifying and resolving problems in the real world. Demonstrations of grasp of a range of practical skills, such as the ability to put problems in context, to transfer and extend information in real-life situations, and collaborate in groups, are capabilities that are seen as able to be monitored, appraised and developed by teaching.

Finally, how the social ratification of the values assigned to these attainments, and how they are related to the attainments of other candidates in other institutions, is seen not as related to an authoritative decision by a powerfully accredited appointee, the moderator, but as derived from a socially constructed consensus arrived at by discussion and interaction in a group of interested users of assessment and moderation. This negotiated consensus needs to be updated regularly as the conditions of life, learning and the needs of users change in an evolving society.

The MAPSW model

In the model, assessment is divided into integrated formative assessment, structured deliberate formative assessment, snap-shot summative assessment and formal structured summative assessment.

Integrated formative assessment

Teachers, in the act of teaching, are engaged in the process of assessing pupils' work. This process is essential in order to determine the development of the pupils' learning achievements. In this sense teachers are constantly assessing and build up a substantial knowledge base about each of their pupils. It could be said that teachers are implicitly using skills of formative assessment, integrated in the teaching process. In other words, no specific assessment instruments are used to disrupt the teaching and learning flow, but teachers are forming judgements about the pupils' ability through observation and response to tasks set.

However, there are occasions when assessment is made more explicit. This focusing on assessment appears to be abstracted out from the teaching context. This can happen in different ways for different purposes but can be categorized broadly in the next three ways.

Structured deliberate formative assessment

This form of assessment concentrates on helping pupils during the process of learning. By its very nature, formative assessment is concerned with supportive measures to help pupils to identify their strengths and weaknesses in learning capabilities and thereby to improve their learning abilities. Teachers and pupils together, consciously and explicitly engage in assessment activities with the purpose of helping the pupils to achieve the learning tasks set. The key feature of formative assessment is to provide guidance to the child through a systematic feedback structure that encourages pupils to take responsibility for their own learning, that is, acquire the skills to plan their learning route to reach agreed objectives.

Snap-shot summative assessment

At a point in time, teachers may decide to give the pupils an assessment in order to sum up where the latter have reached in a particular area and aspect of learning. This is really a reviewing process and is saying: 'It would appear that you know/understand and can do this because that is what the assessment is telling me, so now we can move on to the next stage'. This assessment can take a number of forms. It could be a written test, a piece of written work marked to specific relevant criteria, an oral test or assignment, a demonstration of practical work or a conversational review between teacher and pupil that follows a particular format and looks at the pupil's achievements so far.

All these types of assessing so far described are very much part of the teaching and learning environment that the teachers and the pupils inhabit. Assessing 'checks out' how pupils are learning (formative) or what pupils have learnt (summative) against implicit and/or explicit criteria. Furthermore, it often informs pupils where they are in relation to the achievement of the other pupils in the class.

Formal structured summative assessment

However, assessment does go beyond the confines of the teacher–pupil relationship in the classroom. This category of assessment can be called formal structured summative assessment. This denotes the common assessment instruments that are used by a number of teachers to assess their pupils in different classrooms, in different schools in the same subject/discipline. Although these pupils are taught by different teachers in different ways and in different contexts, this type of assessment is given to denote whether or not all the pupils subject to the assessment have learned what the assessment has been designed to reveal. The assessment could be constructed to show what pupils know/understand and/or do against specified criteria (criterion-referenced assessment) or designed to enable a comparison to be made between pupils in terms of their levels of ability in performing the assessment task (norm-referenced assessment). However, more generally these days it is a mixture of both. It is when assessment reaches this formalized state that it is often seen as synonymous with testing

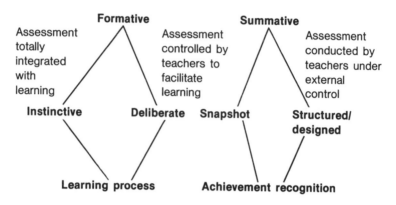

Figure 6.1 Assessment categories

and it is used by the education system to select out pupils of different abilities. These assessments differentiate and discriminate pupils as in the GCSE and will be the function of the National Curriculum SAT. It also provides certification for pupils which denotes the standard reached; in the case of the national assessments at Key Stages 1–3, the attainment level achieved will be recorded. It is true to say that this form of assessment is only part of the assessment picture. It is also the case that all learning that takes place is not necessarily assessed or indeed assessable in a formal structured summative way. The assessment categories described can be diagrammatically presented as in Figure 6.1.

As noted above, formal structured summative assessments rely on common assessment procedures and instruments used by teachers to assess their pupils in different classrooms, in different schools and in the same subject/discipline. Because this commonality is built into the assessment design/instrument these assessments can be moderated. It is because commonality is deliberately built into the assessment design, the procedures, criteria and documentation, that these assessments are open to moderation.

MAPSW takes the view that systematic, structured, efficient, valid and reliable assessments are essential if the process of moderation is to be of value. Hence, we assert that the quality of the moderation activity based on shared understanding is dependent on the quality of the assessment activities. MAPSW has developed assessment principles to aid and support quality assessing which in turn supports quality moderating processes. These are described in the next sub-section.

Assessment principles

1 There must be a clear relationship between the aims of the course and the assessment objectives, of which all, including students, are aware.
2 The assessment objectives must be achievable by the students within the scheme of work devised.
3 The assessment structure must be sound and well designed, that is, must fit the purpose for which it was devised.
4 In practice, the activities undertaken by pupils must be such that the assessment objectives can be met.
5 Assessment processes should be based on clear and understandable criteria that are either context-related or, if general, context-specific examples or interpretations must be always provided.
6 What counts as evidence for assessment purposes must be clearly delineated.
7 Evidence revealed by the students from different sources and in different modes must be equally valued.
8 No assessment statement should be recorded unless evidence for that statement is available and acceptable.

No matter how carefully thought-out the assessment principles are, there is still the probability of different interpretations from different teachers in their own context. Hence the need for moderation which provides the opportunity to compare teachers' marking and grading one with another. It is through comparison of students' work which has been undertaken against agreed criteria that standards are decided and fixed upon. The interpretation of the teachers and moderator together determines the standards. Therefore, moderation is an activity of deliberation and interpretation of information out of which standards are socially constructed.

The key to good moderation practice is the nature of the activity of deliberating about and interpreting information. The significant contributors to the moderation process are: the teachers of the pupils being assessed; and an individual or individuals uninvolved with the pupils whose remit is to place a final value on the pupils' contributions. The research literature, as mentioned earlier in this chapter, has shown that there normally exists a tension between the teachers responsible for coursework assessment and the moderators. This tension can be explained when the perspective that the teachers and the moderators have on the moderation process is taken into account.

Good moderation practice takes positive account of the multiple perspectives that exist within the moderation activity. The teacher perspective is called the 'insider' – that is, the teacher of the pupils being assessed at that point in time. The external assessed perspective is called the 'outsider' – that is, teachers and/or other individuals who have had no teaching contact with the pupils.

The insider perspective

The final assessment of pupils' work by the teacher is the outcome of involvement in the teaching and learning process that both the teacher and the pupils have shared. The teacher's approach to the task is grounded in his or her knowledge of the pupil and overall awareness of pupils' abilities. This knowledge has developed through the integral relationship between the teaching, learning and assessing, both formative and summative, that has been ongoing. The teacher is able to draw on evidence of process skills that form a part of the coursework assessment criteria. Process skills are not necessarily explicitly obvious in the final product presented by the pupil for external assessment. The orientation of teachers is rooted in a holistic view of each of their pupils, and their concern is for a fair and equitable assessment of pupil achievement.

The outsider perspective

The external assessor approaches the business of assessing pupils' work with a very different perspective. As an outsider he or she is separate from the complexities of total immersion in the teaching/assessing process. The outsider orientation is towards placing a value on the attainment and achievement of pupils based on an itemized piece of evidence that has been capable of abstraction

Table 6.1 The 'outsider' and 'insider' perspectives in moderation

Outsider	Insider
Detached from the reality of the context of teaching and learning.	Immersed in the complexities of the contextual reality.
Concerned with monitoring of aspects of knowledge that can be abstracted out of the (whole) coursework.	Involved in a holistic way with knowledge acquisition in relation to particular children.
Has a collective universal notion of attainment and targets – fair and equitable for all pupils.	Is bound up in the realities of interacting with particular children – fair treatment for own cohort.

from the overall learning profile of the pupil. The outsider has a notion of standards of achievement possible for pupils in the particular knowledge area being assessed. This standard is derived from deliberation of samples of pupils' work that are abstracted out of a variety of teaching environments. The holistic notion of the individual child is lost, with the emphasis being placed on the product *per se*.

The insider is involved in a pupil-based process-to-product continuum with the individual pupil central to his or her concerns. The outsider is involved with a product-product continuum, with comparability of pupils central to his or her concerns. In this sense each perspective could inform the other, and the act of moderating could be seen as incorporating the positive aspects of these different perspectives to the benefit of the pupils being assessed. The two perspectives are compared in Table 6.1.

Reconciling the perspectives

The activity of moderation, therefore, is an attempt to reconcile these two different perspectives. The moderation process needs to recognize the outsider–insider dimension in the way it functions in practice. The insider wants his or her own pupils dealt with fairly and the outsider wants to attribute notion of objective standards of the pupils' attainments. The act of moderation recognizes these fundamental tensions and works at reconciling them. The quality of the moderation of pupils' assessments as well as the quality of experience for teachers engaged in the process would be enhanced if the process positively embraced the different perspectives as opposed to ignoring their existence or simply resolving them through the use of power (that is, asserting the external perspective over the internal).

The outsider's stance would be to respect and accept the insider's knowledge, trusting his or her professional judgements of previous stages of assessment that are not open to moderation. In other words, the teacher as assessor is valued. The insider would need to be aware that relating individual work to a notion of generalizable standards is an acceptable part of the process. The outsider's knowledge in this area would act as a catalyst for the interpretations of the insider and enable the pupils' work to be seen in the wider educational context. Outsider information would be used to come to an evaluation of comparability across different teaching environments. In this model it is possible for the teacher to act as both an insider and an outsider at the same meeting, being an 'insider' with regard to his or her own pupils and an 'outsider' with regard to other pupils' work.

Moderation conceived in this way is a supportive system that enables the development of teachers' professionalism in assessment of their pupils' work. The teachers act as equal partners with each other and any outside moderator who may be present. They are able to justify their stances one with another to reach agreement.

Moderation is directly concerned with the quality of the teachers' assessment activities and the teachers' awareness of general standards. Samples of pupils' work are used to achieve this. These samples represent differing levels of quality and cover written, oral and practical work.

Moderation as reconciliation embodies an accountability model that perceives accountability as a two-way process: the more 'objective' assessment establishment, the moderators' officialdom, working in association with the more 'subjective' teacher community to provide a national assessment outcome that reflects actual practice. The model is grounded in reality, based on ongoing dynamic and developing classroom practice, as shown in Figure 6.2.

The strength of the reconciliation model is that, in seeing moderation as integral to the professional capacity and skills of the practising teacher, the process can take place between classroom

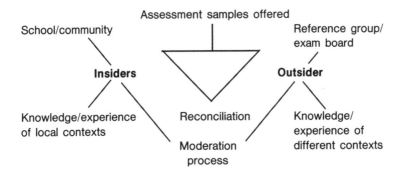

Figure 6.2   The reconciliation model of moderation

teachers, and in schools as well as at consortium and county level. This is because of the recognition of the different perspectives in the process itself.

The reconciliation model in action

The case study that follows starts by describing an 'old' model of moderation that is termed the 'deficit' model, and then goes on to show the positive effect that the reconciliation model has on teacher–moderator relationships.

The deficit model

Teachers come together and, in effect, remark the work of candidates and comparisons are made. The activity is conducted largely in silence because teachers find it difficult to talk, read and mark at the same time. There is an uneasy atmosphere, with a considerable amount of eye movement and looking over the shoulder to see who is marking whose coursework. Each teacher is trying to remark a colleague's work while attempting to keep an eye on the progress, or otherwise, of his or her own materials. There are some verbal exchanges but these are usually of the 'She had glandular fever' or 'His father is in the Middle East' variety, and are not really connected with a discussion of assessment, criteria or evidence. This visual and verbal sharing, coupled with the rapid passing of time, usually aids consensus but the teachers are always placed in a position where they are searching for problems with the marking. The whole atmosphere is one of distrust, fear and uncertainty. Such an approach has been termed the 'deficit model of moderation' by MAPSW ADOs.

Developing the MAPSW model

In one network (of teachers) there was a high degree of consensus during meetings but after the close of official business there were informal 'off-the-record' remarks about some of the outcomes. A network coordinator (and MAPSW ADO) became concerned that these meetings were not really getting anywhere in terms of agreed standards or assessment expertise. The coordinator was also becoming more and more concerned about the number of confidential 'off-the-record' remarks which should have been made at the meeting but were made outside it. Worse still, as an LEA employee the coordinator was being manoeuvred into a position where, at some point, he was going to have to do the work the meeting should have done. If this resulted in the downgrading of some students the coordinator would be left in a delicate situation with a number of possible political repercussions.

The MAPSW assessment and moderation principles were helpful in this respect in that they provided a framework to make sense of assessment and moderation activities in the scheme. A decision was made to replace the 'deficit model' of moderation with the MAPSW reconciliation model and to operationalize the model in a climate of mutual respect, trust, explicitness and professional negotiation. In this way it was hoped that meetings might then become more positive, with teachers having the opportunity to articulate and exchange their subjective interpretations of the criteria, and the moderator able to relate the values that this group assigns to the attainments under discussion with the attainments of other candidates in other networks which would then be able to feed that information into the group. This would mean that the coordinator/moderator would no longer be seen as the decisive powerful accredited appointee but as part of a group of professionals reaching a socially constructed consensus in relation to educational standards.

At the next consensus meeting teacher A used examples of

students' work to outline the reasoning behind a mark of 38 (out of 40), then 30 and then 20 (the insider perspective). Other teachers in the group viewed the work, asked questions and discussed respective interpretations of evidence and criteria (the outsider perspective). Teacher B then did the same. (At coffee-time the teachers stated that they were actually enjoying the exercise!) By the time teacher C was scheduled to make an input a standard was beginning to emerge for a variety of levels (the reconciliation through negotiation of the insider and outsider perspectives). Teacher C's assessments had been those that had given rise to the greatest degree of private concern. Teacher C stated: I'm not sure if I've given this candidate the right mark – I think it might be a bit high.' After discussion, teacher C felt that a number of candidates in the 'upper middle' mark range were perhaps prob- lematic. 'I thought I'd given these candidates high marks but I thought that it was worth a try.'

This last statement is very revealing. Would teacher C have been able to make such a statement in the negative and threatening atmosphere of the 'deficit model'? Had teacher C been playing the 'exam game' until now – applying marks using a norm-referenced rather than criterion-referenced method and then leaving others to make the final decision? (So often we have heard teachers say: 'I'm not sure about this. I'll let the moderator sort it out.') Teachers all the time want to do the best by their own candidates, which is a perfectly understandable feeling. The reconciliation model of moderation does not try to pretend that is not the case but actually builds that concern into the structure of the model. In practice, there is a balance between personal subjective involvement and impersonal objective detachment. In this set-up the teacher is able to juxtapose in a professional manner his or her candidates' attain- ments with other candidates and reach a well-reasoned assessment.

It would seem evident that as teaching and learning styles evolve and become more flexible, so, too, must assessment, moderation and accreditation practices. The use of assessment principles such as those produced by MAPSW, along with a more conciliatory and less threatening moderation model as laid out by the reconciliation model, could do much to aid this process.

Conclusion

The 'new moderation', the reconciliation model of moderation proposed by MAPSW,

- stresses that assessment/moderation is integral with the planning and teaching of courses and continuous with the process of delivery;
- comes from and is responsible to both outside and inside interests in the institution;
- relies on a plurality of judgements brought into agreement by negotiation;
- promotes communication, transfer of information and thus staff development;
- is orientated to quality control and a developmental accountability in partnership;
- signals confidence and trust in teachers;
- and stresses assessment and moderation as a serious management and staff training matter for the school.

At the heart of the new model is the realization that moderation depends on the achievement, by discussion and negotiation within a group, of a socially constructed consensus about how work is to be valued and criteria interpreted.

Our experience over the last three years of MAPSW suggests that many teachers need to update and hone their assessment skills, and even more need to be helped to reflect on moderation procedures and their part in them. Unless training takes place, we believe moderation is likely to revert to an external model which would mean that teachers will be deskilled and the opportunity lost for professional development. In the end delivery of the curriculum will suffer if assessment and moderation are not going to take place in a partnership.

MAPSW grew from a discontent with the limitations of the older assessment/moderation models. We hope that in presenting a model which searches for consensus through reconciliation of viewpoints within an atmosphere of mutual professional respect, teachers, together with others in the educational world, will work towards quality moderation practices to benefit effectively the majority of pupils. For teachers this moderation model holds out the prospect of professional development and eventual accreditation of networks and teachers. This is a model worth disseminating.

Acknowledgements

This chapter is based on the work of the Moderation and Assessment Project-South West (MAPSW) which involved the authors as Director (Hilary Radnor) and Evaluator (Ken Shaw) and the Assessment Development Officers, Chris Leanard, Terry Hunt, Iris Capps, Roy Turner, Tom Banks, Terry Tresize and David Hanson.

7

THE ROLE OF ASSESSMENT IN EDUCATIONAL REFORM

Harry Torrance

Introduction: different perspectives on assessment reform

Using assessment in educational reform seems to be an idea whose time has come. A number of recent publications have drawn attention to the problems and possibilities of using changes in assessment practices to reform education (see, for example, Broadfoot *et al.* 1990; Stake 1991b; Gifford and O'Connor 1992; Office of Technology Assessment 1992); while a recent review of secondary examination by Eckstein and Noah (1993: 9) suggests that this is one of the main reasons why examinations have 'done more than persist' in recent times, but 'have positively flourished'. The idea is perhaps most developed in the United States and the United Kingdom, where professional debates about the merits of measurement-driven instruction, on the one hand (the USA), and direct political intervention on the other (the UK, particularly manifest in the 1988 Education Reform Act), have served to put the relationship of assessment to curriculum change and school reform at the top of the educational policy agenda. However, as Chapter 1 in this volume demonstrates, many other governments are becoming similarly interested in the role of assessment, and other recent publications have also taken up the issues with regard to promoting educational reform in developing countries (Heyneman and Ransom 1992; Kellaghan and Greaney 1992; Lockheed 1992).

Broadly speaking, the argument put forward by proponents of assessment reform is that traditional forms of paper-and-pencil assessment – particularly multiple-choice tests – have a restricting effect on the curriculum and teaching methods and can lead teachers to coach their students in a narrow range of test-taking skills rather than encouraging them to teach a broader range of higher-order competencies and understandings. Thus, by expanding the curriculum content covered by tests and examinations and the range of skills and capabilities tested by them, teachers will be encouraged (or 'driven') to expand their teaching methods and curriculum coverage. Such educational arguments have developed in parallel with more specifically political analyses which argue that setting standards and then setting tests to measure whether or not they have been met will raise levels of educational achievement.

However, while this coincidence of political and educational concern with reforming assessment has certainly created opportunities for change, there is considerable variation in the desired nature and likely consequences of change, and any review of the use of assessment in this context must identify the variety of ways in which such use is being conceptualized and advocated. Certainly the claims and the contributions to debate which publications such as those cited above have made are by no means as uniform as might at first glance appear.

Validity and reliability in selection

Historically, assessment has been developed for purposes of selection and certification – particularly selection for further educational opportunities beyond the minimum of state provision and selection for employment. This has been justified in terms of fairness to individuals, with examinations being seen as constituting as objective a selection mechanism as could be devised, and of appropriateness to the economy whereby the most 'talented' are selected for the most educational investment and thus, so the argument goes, will be able to 'put most back' into the economy. As Heyneman and Ransom (1992: 108) have put it with respect to developing countries: 'examinations can help to ensure that society is investing in those who will in turn make the most useful contributions to society'. This is still a very common perspective, but it begs some severe questions about the effectiveness of schooling in relation to students' social background and about the validity and reliability of examinations for such a purpose. And it is questions of validity in particular which constitute one point of departure for current debates about assessment, since narrow test procedures may not only have a narrowing effect on the curriculum, but also result in the 'wrong' candidates succeeding – those who are good at test-taking rather than those who 'will in turn make the most useful contributions to society'. Of course, it is extremely difficult to tease out cause and effect in such circumstances, but it is important to note that using assessment in educational reform can and probably still will involve its use as a mechanism for selection, and, in the UK at least, as indicated in Chapters 2, 4 and 6 in this volume, interest in changing assessment methods has been stimulated by a combination of interests in broadening the curriculum and making assessment results more valid indicators of a wider range of educational achievement. Thus change has been pursued for reasons of equity, to make examinations fairer, as well as economic efficiency, to make examinations more relevant and effective selection mechanisms.

System monitoring and management

Exactly what change should involve, and how the relationship between assessment and schooling should be conceptualized, is also a matter of debate. Perceptions of the differing role(s) that assessment could play in educational reform span a continuum from seeing assessment purely in terms of its products, its results, and the use to which results might be put in managing or even driving school systems, through to seeing assessment as a process, almost wholly integrated with teaching, such that improvements in assessment means improvements in the process of teaching and learning at classroom level.

Thus, for example, the role of assessment can be conceived of purely in terms of using results for purposes of national monitoring and system management. This is a fairly common role (cf. Nuttall 1993), though is achieved by a variety of different means and strategies. It is also a role which can be operationalized at local as well as national level, and accomplished through the analysis of already existing data (for example, individual examination results) or through the generation of new data, such as that produced by national monitoring programmes like the US National Assessment of Educational Progress (NAEP) or the UK Assessment of Performance Unit (APU).

The production of new data usually involves light sampling of the curriculum as well as the student population and clearly can only indicate overall trends rather than identifying specific problems for potentially remedial action. It also suffers from being a 'low stakes' test situation, that is, one that carries few if any consequences for the individual test-takers and their teachers and therefore is unlikely to draw forth highly motivated best performances. In turn, therefore, the data derived from such an exercise may not constitute a particularly valid indicator of educational achievement.

Examination results, by contrast, represent 'high stakes' data which do carry consequences and the analysis of which should be able to indicate appropriate follow-up action, especially if results are analysed in sufficient detail to indicate the ways in which individual schools are making more or less of a difference to the achievements of particular groups of students. Thus such analysis could indicate schools that were doing particularly well (and thus might be worthy of study in order to identify and disseminate what they are doing so effectively) or schools that were doing particularly badly and may be in need of specific support. Such a model, however, and indeed the light sampling model as well, takes no view of the possible impact of assessment on the curriculum and/or teaching as such. Indeed, in the light sampling version of monitoring steps have been taken quite deliberately to avoid impact on the curriculum since this was regarded as a potentially undesirable side-effect of the research design (Wood and Power 1984). Nor can the analysis of results in itself generate information about why trends are moving in one direction or another, or why one school seems to be more effective than its neighbour; this would require further investigation. Rather, the model is predicated on the assumption that the examinations or tests in question are valuable and significant indicators of educational achievement and quality, and that the overall system can be managed on the basis of such indicators by, for example, informing future resource allocation decisions, or by inspectors following up problems in individual schools, or, indeed, by some combination of the two.

Thus for example Lockheed's (1992) recent review of the role of assessment in a developing country context treats educational assessment as a form of applied research. Although she also identifies current World Bank projects which involve changing the examination systems of particular countries, her review focuses on the use of assessment results as evaluation data through which the effectiveness of developing systems can be monitored. From this system-monitoring and evaluation perspective, impact on schools and teaching would arise through strategic management decisions about the allocation of resources and so on being taken on the basis of analysed test results.

Standard setting and accountability

A more aggressively interventionist version of the same model *would* take a view about the impact of assessment on teaching and would involve some attempt to define minimum standards or set 'benchmarks' of what children should be able to achieve at certain ages. Such intervention could also occur in the context of accountability legislation which involves the publication of test results and the movement of students from school to school with finance following the students. This impact is still considerably removed from classroom processes, however. Rather, the assumption (and it is a particularly mechanistic one) seems to be that simply by setting certain standards, testing regularly and publishing results, teachers will inevitably change their practice, and that change will involve improvement. Such an assumption begs some severe questions about how standards are defined, how they are translated into test specifications, and whether teachers can change so easily. As Stake (1991b: xxiv–xxv) has put it:

> One key assumption behind reform based on assessment policy is that people can agree on which educational outcomes

are desirable . . . A second assumption is that we have a language for the specification of educational goals . . . A third assumption is that we can measure the attainment of those [goals] . . . A fourth assumption is that . . . we can use the information to improve teaching.

Such aspirations have also fallen foul of considerable empirical evidence which suggests that minimum standards or minimum competency often become a *de facto* maximum as teachers strive to make sure all students reach the minimum, rather than stretching some well beyond it. Similarly, coaching and practice can lead to improvements in test results without any real or lasting improvement on educational quality (Atkin 1979; Corbett and Wilson 1988; Shepard 1991).

When operationalized in certain accountability settings such a model also has other drawbacks. Schools can only take in new students up to a workable maximum – schools cannot expand (or contract) indefinitely. In such circumstances popular schools are likely to end up selecting students, rather than vice versa, with many unpredictable consequences for motivation and quality of provision for students who are not selected. Unpopular schools cannot continue to decline in numbers without severe implications for the standard of educational provision for their remaining students.

Also the most ambitious of such schemes, such as the national curriculum and assessment programme of England and Wales, raise many issues with respect to logistics and manageability. Instituting periodic national testing in the context of nationally prescribed 'attainment targets' for every school student will certainly have a direct impact on schools and classrooms, but it involves a massive investment in test development and teacher and student time. The UK experience, reported in previous chapters, is that the imperative of scale undermines any aspiration to broaden the scope and quality of assessment, and leaves us with a system essentially geared to market accountability as the mechanism for school improvement, rather than improvements in teaching being brought about by improvements in assessment *per se*.

Improving the curriculum and teaching

Improving the curriculum and teaching methods through improving assessment methods probably represents the most ambitious educational perspective on developments at the present time. This aspiration is at the heart of the debate outlined in the Introduction to this volume and pervades all of the other contributions to the volume in one way or another. Here the focus is very much on the curriculum and the classroom. As Resnick and Resnick (1992: 59) argue: 'if we put debates, discussions, essays and problem solving into the testing system, children will spend time practicing those activities'. Heyneman and Ransom (1992: 110–11) make similar claims with regard to expanding the content of tests to encompass 'the ability to observe, experiment and interpret, to understand concepts and reasoned conclusions, to use knowledge and skills to solve problems and make decisions in new situations'.

However, as we have seen from the various contributions to this book, this is easier said than done, particularly in a political atmosphere dominated by the concerns of accountability. Using authentic assessment to reform schooling raises issues concerning how, and by whom, new educational goals are to be identified, how they are to be encapsulated in the design of new assessments, how those designs are to be operationalized, whether or not teachers are sufficiently aware of and skilled in the pursuit of new goals, and, if not, what sort of training and material support might be provided for them (and, once again, by whom). In addition, the coincidence of educational and political interest in developing assessment methods and procedures for new purposes raises as many problems as it solves when it comes to implementation and impact. As Shepard (1992: 326) has noted:

> The idea that accountability requires testing every pupil in every grade in every subject has to be given up to make it feasible to institute performance assessments. It should be clear for logistical reasons that the same assessment cannot be used for instructional purposes and for accountability to external audiences.

Unfortunately, the British experience has been that it is the accountability purposes which survive such logistical tensions. The testing regime which is emerging in Britain is much lighter than initially envisaged (see the Introduction to this volume) but this has been achieved by a combination of cutting down on the number of subjects to be tested *and* cutting down on the scope of the tests. The numbers of students being tested has remained the same – every child at ages 7, 11, 14 and 16. The concomitant dangers of narrowing the curriculum to what is being tested remains a very real possibility, although the role of teacher assessment in other subjects and for the broader range of 'attainment targets' in tested subjects, also remains as a potential counter to a curriculum dominated by testing. However, while school-based teacher assessment might preserve flexibility in teaching and curriculum provision, it cannot 'drive' it in that direction. The sorts of educational goals outlined by Resnick and Resnick, and Heyneman and Ransom, above, are increasingly *not* being represented in the Standard Tests of the UK national assessment programme; they are being left to be pursued and assessed by teachers as part of their normal classroom teaching and coursework. Whether or not this happens depends on the curriculum prescriptions to which the teachers are working, whether or not they feel they have the time and material resources to pursue such goals, and whether they receive in-service support and encouragement to do so.

Teaching and learning in the classroom

This brings us on to what might be termed the final 'level' at which assessment, and particularly authentic assessment, can impact on the educational process: that of teacher–student interaction and the impact of assessment on learning. As noted in the Introduction to this volume, diagnostic assessment has a long history and clearly carries implications for teaching in so far as teachers will be using the information generated to modify their teaching and perhaps set in train some sort of remedial programme. Particular grouping decisions and/or guidance for individual students can also be based on such assessment. However, such assessment can be of a fairly traditional type, albeit at a considerable level of detail and perhaps pursued with individual students through the medium of speech rather than the written word.

Implementing authentic assessment at this level of the system

would involve a much more interactive and constructivist approach
to teaching, learning and assessment being taken with all children,
rather than just the apparent underachievers. Current developments in the field of linguistics and social psychology are focusing
on the processes of learning and how they can be 'scaffolded'
(Bruner 1985), that is to say, how young children in particular
can be supported in the process of learning by appropriate teacher
(or peer) intervention. As O'Connor (1992: 19) has put it: 'The
focus in . . . cognitive science . . . is to better understand the
learner . . . and thus to improve the ability of schools to foster
learning and development.' The process of scaffolding in itself will
depend on teachers making judgements – formative assessments –
about not only what a child has achieved but also what he or she
might now be ready to achieve. Such formative assessment may
involve setting children specific tests or tasks but if it is to be
integrated into the everyday routines of teaching it will rest far
more on detailed observation and questioning of children by their
teachers. Thus the planning of teaching, the conduct of teaching,
and the naturalistic observation of students on task, would constitute the full integration of teaching with assessment. Certainly
this seems to be the aspiration of at least some of the proponents
of formative teacher assessment within the British national assessment system (cf. SEAC 1990; Torrance 1993a). However, such a
practice implies developing teacher skills in assessment at school
level with reference to theories of learning, rather than developing
better tests *outside* of schools and then implementing them in
order to influence teaching. This is a rather different enterprise to
what some might consider to be the appropriate focus of authentic
assessment, though it once again begs many similar questions of
feasibility and professional development, as noted in Chapter 3 in
this volume.

Discussion

Kellaghan and Greaney (1992) have produced a very thorough
review of the costs, benefits, problems and possible unintended
consequences of examination reform. As well as drawing attention
to the range of practical difficulties that attempts at reform would
face (particularly with regard to resources and teacher skills)

ambiguities in such evidence as we have about examination reform are also acknowledged. Thus even the desirability of examination reform is questioned, as well as its feasibility. In the end, however, Kellaghan and Greaney (1992: 65) conclude that

> unreformed examination systems are likely to cause damage to the quality of education offered in schools. It obviously makes sense to take steps to change such systems and to develop examinations which are more in keeping with principles of good assessment practice.

This still raises questions about the nature and scope of such development, of course, and in reviewing the various 'levels' at which it might be hoped that changes in assessment could lead to improvements in schooling we have identified a number of issues to do with defining and delineating what the task should actually entail, how ambitious the goals of policy-makers should be, and what process of development and implementation might be most effective. Aspirations range from attempting to use test results to inform system management, to an aspiration directly to influence teaching and learning in individual classrooms and in particularly complex directions. Within debates about the efficacy of combining authentic assessment with attempts to drive the curriculum in particular directions, one can also imagine various 'staging posts' or 'half-way houses' whereby the inclusion of practical tests in addition to paper-and-pencil tests, and/or more sophisticated questions testing understanding in addition to the recall of knowledge, might have a less detailed but still significant impact on curricula and achievement – cf. Madaus and Kellaghan's (1992) discussion of the inclusion of practical tests in military training.

Two basic perspectives seem to emerge from this review, however: that of using assessment *results* to influence or manage the system in some way; and that of using changes in assessment *processes* to improve teaching directly by providing exemplary models of what good teaching and assessment tasks should look like. Thus, is the concern of reformers with system monitoring (a goal which could also be achieved through judicious sampling) or with directly changing the curricular provision of all students in some or all year groups?

If it is system monitoring, questions are still begged about how acceptable objectives and levels of achievement are to be defined, whether existing examinations are to be relied upon or whether, and if so how, new tests are to be designed and conducted, and how best use can be made of the resulting information. This latter point is particularly important since it is the *raison d'être* of the approach. Even supposing that we can learn something valid and reliable about what is happening, this does not in itself tell us how or why it is happening or what to do about it. Qualitative data are required for school *improvement* as distinct from monitoring school and system effectiveness. The experience of the APU with this sort of monitoring was that results were seized upon by the popular press if they seemed poor, were largely ignored if they seemed good, and in any case there was no overall management system in place to act upon them either way. Any impact on standards took place over a relatively long period of time (ten years or more) as the lessons learned about student achievement and the new assessment techniques which the Unit developed were disseminated through initial and in-service training, the mediating influence of local authority advisory services, and in turn were incorporated in various ways into GCSE and the National Curriculum.

If our interest is in direct intervention in curricular provision, then questions are begged about the nature and scope of this intervention. Is the intention to change curriculum content, or teaching methods, or both? To an extent, of course, any change in content will imply some change in method, but clearly there are degrees of emphasis which need to be considered particularly if the desire is to develop more practical work, oral work, group work and so forth. In turn, decisions need to be taken about whether the change is to be a relatively broad one – introducing practical tests into a system which does not at present use them, or perhaps increasing the weighting of existing practical tests – or is to be more ambitious, seeking to influence the detail of teacher–student interaction through providing novel and exemplary assessment tasks or even prescribing the teacher role in the assessment process. Whatever is the case, considerable attention will have to be paid to teacher preparedness – the deskilling and reskilling which such changes will imply – and to the provision of dissemination mechanisms and in-service support. Likewise, the provision of resources at school level for new activities and new methods of teaching will have to be considered. Developing more practical and investigative work in science and technology is likely to carry particular implications in this respect.

As regards implementation, evidence from the UK reviewed in previous chapters suggests that changes in assessment and especially public examinations impact most positively on curriculum and teaching methods when the intention that they should do so is made explicit and when teachers have an active role in the development process. There is no straightforward mechanistic relationship between assessment and curriculum, and just because poor assessment can narrow the curriculum and depress standards, it does not follow that better assessment will automatically enhance the curriculum and raise standards. Crude changes in curriculum content and teaching methods can be instigated, but the quality of these changes will depend on teacher perceptions of their purpose and understandings of their broader curricular intentions. This carries implications for the sort of in-service support which is provided to assist the process of change and the sort of time-scale which we might have in mind for successful implementation. Thus, for example, even when GCSE was introduced with an explicit focus on curriculum development, most teachers were initially concerned to be clear about their role as assessors. The paradigm or perspective of 'assessment', as opposed to 'teaching', framed the way in which they interpreted the innovation and their role within it. This was compounded by the examination boards being charged with responsibility for organizing in-service training and so, as Chapter 2 in this volume makes clear, the main topics of concern, at least to begin with, were the criteria and procedures for assessment, rather than curriculum improvement.

Eckstein and Noah's (1993) recent review of secondary school examinations argues that designing assessment systems will always involve policy-makers in a variety of educational and political trade-offs. They conclude that:

> while reform of the testing and examination system is quite properly regarded as a way to lever education to a higher level of performance . . . policymakers constantly need to be mindful of the likelihood of unintended, undesirable consequences of their decision.
>
> (Eckstein and Noah 1993: 16)

The research reported in this book certainly bears out this

conclusion and more. The aspiration to use changes in assessment to reform education involves an implicit (and sometimes explicit) aspiration to have an impact on each and every teacher and pupil in the system. This cannot be done directly except by compromising on the quality of the assessment design. The larger the scope of the assessment programme, the narrower the design of the assessment tasks is likely to be. This may not trouble policy-makers who are first and foremost interested in accountability and have a belief in raising standards through competition, but it ought to, since it returns us to where we started in terms of the potentially negative consequences of narrow programmes of assessment on the quality of learning and achievement.

Similarly, however, educational advocates of extending authentic assessment in order to influence teaching have to address issues of scale and interpretation of the enterprise by teachers at classroom level. The larger the programme, the more distant is its genesis likely to be from individual schools and classrooms. The more it concentrates on test development (however authentic) rather than curriculum change, the more likely is its purpose to be interpreted in terms of the validity and reliability of test results, rather than the improvement of teaching and learning. Effective developments in this field are likely to involve the dissemination of principles and exemplary material from central development teams, but they will also require extensive scope for local adaptation, development and implementation in order to explore the curricular implications and potential of the innovation. The evidence from this book is that improvements in assessment may be a necessary but are by no means a sufficient condition to bring about improvements in teaching.

REFERENCES

Airasian, P. W. (1988) Measurement-driven instruction: a closer look, *Educational Measurement: Issues and Practice* 7(4): 6–11.

Atkin M. (1979) Educational accountability in the United States, *Educational Analysis* 1(1): 5–21.

Australian Educational Council (1989) Report of the Working Party on Basic Skills and Program Evaluation (including student portfolios) cited in Masters, G. (1990) *Subject Profiles as Frameworks for Assessing and Reporting Student Achievement*. Discussion paper for Management Committee of Australian Co-operative Assessment Project, Perth.

Ball, S. and Bowe, R. (1992) 'Subject departments and the "implementation" of the National Curriculum'. *Journal of Curriculum Studies* 24(2): 97–115.

Bennett, S. N., Wragg, E. C., Carre, C. G. and Carter, D. S. G. (1992) A longitudinal study of primary teachers' perceived competence in, and concerns about, National Curriculum implementation, *Research Papers in Education* 7(1).

Bennetts, J. (1986) The moderation of teacher assessment, *Education in Science* 120: 16–18.

Black, H. and Dockrell, W. B. (1984) *Criterion-Referenced Assessment in the Classroom*. Edinburgh: Scottish Council for Research in Education.

Black, H., Hale, J., Martin, S. and Yates, J. (1989) *The Quality of*

Assessment. Edinburgh: Scottish Council for Research in Education.

Bracey, G. (1987) Measurement-driven instruction: catchy phrase, dangerous practice, *Phi Delta Kappan* 68: 683–6.

Broadfoot, P. (1992) Assessment procedures in French education, *Education Review* 44(3): 309–26.

Broadfoot, P. and Osborn, M. (1986) Teachers' conceptions of their professional responsibility: some international comparisons. Paper presented at BERA conference, Bristol.

Broadfoot, P., James, M., McMeeking, S., Nuttall, D. and Stierer, B. (1988) *Records of Achievement: Report of the National Evaluation of Pilot Schemes*. London: HMSO.

Broadfoot, P., Murphy, R. and Torrance, H. (eds) (1990) *Changing Educational Assessment: International Perspectives and Trends*. London: Routledge.

Broadfoot, P., Harlen, W., Gipps, C. and Nuttall, D. (1992) Assessment and the improvement of education, *The Curriculum Journal* 13(3): 215–30.

Brown, A. and Ferrara, R. (1985) Diagnosing zones of proximal development. In J. Wertsch (ed.) *Culture, Communication and Cognition: Vygotskian Perspectives*. Cambridge: Cambridge University Press.

Brown, A., Campione, J., Webber, L. and McGilly, K. (1992) Interactive learning environments: a new look at assessment and instruction. In B. Gifford and M. O'Connor (eds) *Future Assessments: Changing Views of Aptitude, Achievement and Instruction*. Boston: Kluwer.

Brown, M. (1989) The Graded Assessment in Mathematics Project. In D. F. Robitaille (ed.) *Evaluation and Assessment in Mathematics*, Science and Technology Education Series No. 32. Paris: Unesco.

Brown, M. (1992) Elaborate nonsense? The muddled tale of SATs in mathematics at KS3. In C. V. Gipps (ed.) *Developing Assessment for the National Curriculum*, Bedford Way Series, University of London Institute of Education. London: Kogan Page.

Bruner, J. (1985) 'Vygotsky: a historical and conceptual perspective' in Wertsch, J. (ed.) *Culture, Communication and Cognition: Vygotskian Perspectives*. Cambridge: Cambridge University Press.

Burke, J. and Jessup, G. (1990) Assessment in NVQs: disentangling validity from reliability. In T. Horton (ed.) *Assessment Debates*. London: Hodder & Stoughton.

Clarke, L. and Wolf, A. (1991) Blue Badge Guides: Assessment of national knowledge requirements. Final Project Report to the Department of Employment (unpublished).

Cohen, D. K. and Spillane, J. P. (1992) Policy and practice: the relations between governance and instruction, *Review of Research in Education* 18: 3–49.

Cole, N. S. (1990) Conceptions of educational achievement, *Educational Research* 19(3): 2–7.

Cooper, M. (1988) Whose culture is it anyway? In A. Lieberman (ed.) *Building a Professional Culture in Schools*. New York: Teachers College Press.

Corbett, H. and Wilson, B. (1988) Raising the stakes in statewide mandatory minimum-competency testing. *Journal of Education Policy* 3(5): 27–39.

Crookes, T. (1993) *New Zealand National Education Monitoring Project*. University of Otago.

Dearing, R. (1994) *The National Curriculum and its Assessment*. London: School Curriculum and Assessment Authority.

Department for Education (1992) *Assessment arrangements for KS1 in 1993* (Circular 12/92). London: Department for Education, 19 August.

Department of Education and Science (1985a) *General Certificate of Secondary Education: A General Introduction*. London: HMSO.

Department of Education and Science (1985b) *GCSE General Criteria*. London: HMSO.

Department of Education and Science (1992) *The Parent's Charter: Publication of Information about School Performance in 1992*. (Circular 7/92). London: DES, 19 June.

Edgeworth, F. Y. (1890) The element of chance in competitive examinations, *Proceedings of the Royal Statistical Society*, 461–75 and 644–63.

Eckstein, M. and Noah, H. (1993) *A Comparative Study of Secondary School Examinations*, Research Working Paper No. 7. London: International Centre for Research on Assessment.

Filer, A. (1993) Contexts of assessment in a primary classroom, *British Educational Research Journal* 19(1): 95–107.

Fredericksen, J. R. and Collins, A. (1989) A systems approach to educational testing, *Educational Researcher* 8(9): 27–32.

Fullan, M. (1991) *The New Meaning of Educational Change*. London: Cassell.

Galton, M., Simon, B. and Croll, P. (1980) *Inside the Primary Classroom*. London: Routledge & Kegan Paul.

Gifford, B. and O'Connor, M. (eds) (1992) *Future Assessments: Changing Views of Aptitude, Achievement and Instruction*. Boston: Kluwer.

Gipps, C. V. (ed.) (1986) *The GCSE: An Uncommon Examination*. University of London, Bedford Way Papers No. 29.

Gipps, C. V. (1992) *National Testing at Seven: what can it tell us?* Paper present to AERA 1992 San Francisco.

Gipps, C. V. (1994 in press) *Beyond Testing. Towards a Theory of Educational Assessment*. London: Falmer.

Gipps, C. V., Steadman, S., Goldstein, H. and Stierer, B. (1983) *Testing Children*. London: Heinemann Educational Press.

Gipps, C. V., McCallum, B., McAllister, S. and Brown, M. (1992) National assessment at 7: some emerging themes. In C. V. Gipps (ed.) *Developing Assessment for the National Curriculum*, Bedford Way Series, University of London Institute of Education. London: Kogan Page.

Glaser, B. G. and Strauss, A. L. (1967) *The Discovery of Grounded Theory*. Chicago: Aldine.

Goldstein, H. (1992) *Reconceptualising Mental Measurement*, ICRA Working Paper No. 2. London: University of London Institute of Education.

Good, F. and Cresswell, M. (1988) *Grading the GCSE*. London: Secondary Examinations Council.

Grant, M. (1989) *GCSE in Practice: Managing Assessment Innovation*. Windsor: NFER-Nelson.

Harlen, W. (1993) How do SATs and TA measure up? *Primary Science Review* 26(February).

Harlen, W. and Qualter, A. (1991) Issues in SAT development and the practice of teacher assessment, *Cambridge Journal of Education* 21(2).

Harlen, W., Gipps, C. V., Broadfoot, P. and Nuttall, D. (1992) Assessment and the improvement of education. *The Curriculum Journal* 3(3).

Hewitt, R. (1991) *GCSE Oral Communication Assessment and Inter-Ethnic Variation – A Report to the ESRC*. London: Social Science Research Unit, University of London Institute of Education.

Heyneman, S. and Ransom, A. (1992) Using examinations and testing to improve educational quality. In M. Eckstein and H. Noah (eds) *Examinations: Comparative and International Studies*. Oxford: Pergamon.

Her Majesty's Inspectorate (1992) *The Implementation of the Curricular Requirements of the Education Reform Act. Assessment, Recording and Reporting*. London: HMSO.

Hodkinson, P. (1990) NCVQ and the 16–19 curriculum, *British Journal of Education and Work* 4(3): 25–8.

Horton, T. (ed.) (1987) *GCSE: Examining the New System*. London: Harper & Row.

House, E. (1974) *The Politics of Educational Innovation*. Berkeley, CA: McCutchan.

Huberman, M. and Miles, M. (1984) *Innovation Up Close*. New York: Plenum.

Inner London Education Authority (1984) *Improving Secondary Schools* (The Hargreaves Report). London: ILEA.

James, M. and Conner, C. (1993) Are reliability and validity achievable in National Curriculum assessment? Some observations on moderation at key stage one in 1992, *The Curriculum Journal* 4(1).

Jessup, G. (1991) *Outcomes: NVQs and the Emerging Model of Education and Training*. London: Falmer Press.

Kellaghan, T. and Greaney, V. (1992) *Using Examinations to Improve Education*. Washington, DC: World Bank.

Kempa, R. (1986) *Assessment in Science*. Cambridge: Cambridge University Press.

Koretz, D., Linn, R., Dunbar, S. and Shepard, L. (1991) *The effects of high-stakes testing on achievement: preliminary findings about generalization across tests*. Paper presented to American Educational Research Association/National Council for Measurement in Education.

Koretz, D. Stecher, B. and Deibert, E. (1992) *The Vermont Portfolio Assessment Program: Interim Report on Implementation and Impact 1991–2 School Year*. CSE Technical Report 350, Los Angeles: University of California.

Linn, R. L. (1992) *Linking results of distinct assessments*. Unpublished paper, August.

Linn, R. L. (1993) Educational assessment: expanded expectations and challenges. *Educational Evaluation and Policy Analysis* 15(1).

Linn, R., Baker, E. and Dunbar, S. (1991) Complex, performance-based assessment: expectations and validation criteria, *Educational Researcher* 20(8): 15–21

Lockheed, M. (1992) *World Bank Support for Capacity Building: The Challenge of Educational Assessment*. Washington, DC: World Bank.

MacDonald, B. (1974) Evaluation and the control of education. In R. Murphy and H. Torrance (eds) (1987) *Evaluating Education: Issues and Methods*. London: Harper & Row.

Madaus, G. and Kellaghan, T. (1992) Curriculum evaluation and assessment. In P. Jackson (ed.) *Handbook of Research on Curriculum*. New York: Macmillan.

Marris, P. (1975) *Loss and Change*. New York: Anchor Press/Doubleday.

Masters, G. (1990) Subject profiles as frameworks for assessing and reporting student achievement. Mimeo: Australian Council for Educational Research.

McCallum, B., Gipps, C., McAlister, S. and Brown, M. (1993) *The impact and use of national assessment at seven*. Paper presented at British Educational Research Association Conference, Liverpool.

Mehrens, W. (1992) Using performance assessment for accountability purposes, *Educational Measurement: Issues & Practice* 2(1): 3–9.

Messick, S. (1989) 'Validity' in R. L. Linn (ed.) *Educational Measurement*, 3rd edn. New York: ACE/NCME, Macmillan.

Ministry of Education, Victoria (1991) (Schools Programs Division) *Literacy Profiles Handbook, Curriculum Frameworks Support Materials*. Victoria: Ministry of Education.

Ministry of Education, Western Australia (1990) *Monitoring Standards in Education Information Bulletins*. Perth: Ministry of Education.

Moss, P. A. (1992) Shifting conceptions of validity in educational measurement: implications for performance assessment, *Review of Educational Research* 62(3): 229–58.

Murphy, R. (1978) Reliability of marking in 8 GCE exams, *British Journal of Psychology*, 48: 196–200.

Murphy, R. (1982) Further report of investigations into the reliability of marking of GCE exams, *British Journal of Psychology*, 52: 28–63.

Murphy, R. and Torrance, H. (1988) *The Changing Face of Educational Assessment*. Milton Keynes: Open University Press.

National Council for Vocational Qualifications (1991) *Guide to National Vocational Qualifications*. London: NCVQ.

NFER/BGC (1991) *An Evaluation of National Curriculum Assessment* Report 3. June 1991. London: School Examinations and Assessment Council.

NFER/BGC (1992) *An Evaluation of the 1992 National Curriculum Assessment at KSI* Sept 1992. London: School Examinations and Assessment Council.

New Zealand Ministry of Education 'Tomorrow's Standards: Report of the Ministerial Working Party on Assessment for Better Learning'. Wellington: New Zealand Ministry of Education.

Nias, J. (1989) *Primary Teachers Talking*. London: Routledge.

Nickerson, R. S. (1989) New directions in educational assessment, *Educational Researcher* 18(9): 3–7.

Nisbet, J. (ed.) (1992) *Assessment and Curriculum Reform*. University of Aberdeen.

Northern Ireland Schools Examinations and Assessment Council (1992) Assessment Arrangements for 1992/3 Pilot Year. Belfast: NISEAC.

Nuttall, D. (1987) 'The Validity of Assessments'. *European Journal of Psychology of Education*, 11(2): 109–118.

Nuttall, D. (1993) *Monitoring National Standards*, Research Working Paper No. 6. London, International Centre for Research on Assessment.

O'Connor, M. (1992) Rethinking aptitude, achievement and instruction: cognitive science research and the framing of assessment policy. In B. Gifford and M. O'Connor (eds) *Future Assessments: Changing Views of Aptitude, Achievement and Instruction*. Boston: Kluwer.

Office of Technology Assessment (Congress of the United States) (1992) *Testing in American Schools: Asking the Right Questions* (summary report). Washington, DC: OTA.

Orr, L. and Nuttall, D. L. (1983) *Determining Standards in the Proposed Single System of Examining at 16+*. London: Schools Council.

Pennycuick, D. (1988) 'The Development, Use and Impact of Graded

Tests' in Murphy, R. and Torrance, H. *The Changing Face of Educational Assessment*. Buckingham: Open University Press.

Pennycuick, D. and Murphy, R. (1988) *The Impact of Graded Tests*. London: Falmer Press.

Peterson, J. (1992) *A case study evaluation of the implementation of GCSE*. PhD thesis, University of Sussex.

Pluvinage, F. (1992) L'Evaluation dans la gestion des enseignements: commentaires sur l'evaluation 1991 en sixième. Paper given to 15th CESE Congress, Dijon.

Pole, C. (1993) *Assessing and Recording Achievement*. Milton Keynes: Open University Press.

Pollard, A. (ed.) (1987) *Children and their Primary Schools*. London: Falmer Press.

Pollard, A., Broadfoot, P., Croll, P., Osborn, M. and Abbott, D. (1994) *Changing English Primary Schools*. London: Cassells.

Popham, W. J. (1987) The merits of measurement-driven instruction, *Phi Delta Kappan*, 68: 679–82.

Prais, S. (1991) Vocational qualifications in Britain and Europe: theory and practice, *National Institute Economic Review*, 136: 86–92.

Radnor, H. (1987) *The Impact of the Introduction of GCSE at LEA and School Level*. Slough: NFER.

Resnick, L. and Resnick, D. P. (1992) Assessing the thinking curriculum. In B. Gifford and M. O'Connor (eds), *Future Assessments: Changing Views of Aptitude, Achievement and Instruction*. Boston: Kluwer.

Rowland, S. (1987) An interpretative model of teaching and learning. In A. Pollard (ed.) *Children and their Primary Schools*. London: Falmer Press.

Sadler, R. (1987) Specifying and promulgating achievement standards, *Oxford Review of Education* 13: 191–209.

Schools Council (1977) *Assessment by Teachers in Examinations at 16+*. London: Evans Methuen Educational.

Schools Examination and Assessment Council (1989) *National Curriculum Assessment Arrangements* (SEAC's advice to the Secretary of State, 12.12.89). London: SEAC.

Schools Examination and Assessment Council (1990) *A Guide to Teacher Assessment, Packs A, B & C*. London: Heinemann Educational.

Schools Examination and Assessment Council (1991) *Coursework: Learning from the GCSE Experience*. London: SEAC.

Schools Examination and Assessment Council (1991) *National Curriculum Assessment at Key Stage 3: A Review of the 1991 Pilot with Implications for 1992*. Evaluation & Monitoring Unit: SEAC.

Secondary Examinations Council (1985) *Coursework Assessment in GCSE*. London: SEC.

Secondary Examinations Council (1986) *Policy and Practice in School-based Assessment*, Working Paper 3. London: SEC.

Secondary Examinations Council (1988) *Managing GCSE Coursework in Schools and Colleges*, Working Paper 6. London: SEC.

Shavelson, R., Baxter, G. and Pine, J. (1992) Performance assessments: political rhetoric and measurement reality, *Educational Researcher* 21(4).

Shepard, L. (1991) Will national tests improve student learning?, *Phi Delta Kappan* 71, 232–8.

Shepard, L. (1992) What policymakers who mandate tests should know about the new psychology of intellectual ability and learning. In B. Gifford and M. O'Connor (eds) *Future Assessments: Changing Views of Aptitude, Achievement and Instruction*. Boston: Kluwer.

Shorrocks, D., Daniels, S., Frobisher, L., Nelson, N., Waterson, A. and Bell, J. (1992) *ENCA Project*. London: SEAC.

Stake, R. E. (1991a) The teacher, standardised testing and prospects of revolution, *Phi Delta Kappan* 71, 243–7.

Stake, R. (ed.) (1991b) *Advances in Program Evaluation, Using Assessment Policy to Reform Education*. Greenwich, CT: JAI Press.

Stiggins, R. J. (1992) Two disciplines of educational assessment, *Counselling and Development*.

Swain, M. (1990) Second Language Testing & Second Language Acquisition: Is there a conflict with traditional psychometrics? Georgetown University: 1990.

Task Group on Assessment and Testing (1988) *Task Group on Assessment and Testing: A Report*. London: DES.

Thomson, G. and Ward, K. (1992) Test material and its use in the primary school. University of Edinburgh.

Times Educational Supplement (1993) 'Dunce City' leads league table battle, *TES*, 28 February: 8.

Torrance, H. (1982) *Mode III Examining: Six Case Studies*. York, Longman for the Schools Council.

Torrance, H. (1984) School-based examining: a mechanism for school-based professional development and accountability, *British Educational Research Journal* 10(1): 71–81.

Torrance, H. (1986a) Expanding school-based assessment: issues, problems and future possibilities, *Research Papers in Education* 1(1): 48–59.

Torrance, H. (1986b) School based assessment in GCSE: aspirations, problems and possibilities. In C. Gipps (ed.) *The GCSE: An Uncommon Examination*. University of London, Bedford Way Papers No. 29.

Torrance, H. (ed.) (1988) *National Assessment and Testing: A Research Response*. Kendal: British Educational Research Association.

Torrance, H. (1989) Theory, practice and politics in the development of assessment, *Cambridge Journal of Education* 19: 183–91.

Torrance, H. (1991a) Evaluating SATs: the 1990 pilot, *Cambridge Journal of Education* 21(2): 129–40.

Torrance, H. (1991b) Records of achievement and formative assessment: some complexities of practice. In R. Stake (ed.) *Advances in Program Evaluation, Using Assessment Policy to Reform Education*. Greenwich, CT: JAI Press.

Torrance, H. (1993a) Formative assessment: some theoretical problems and empirical questions, *Cambridge Journal of Education* 23(3): 333–43.

Torrance, H. (1993b) Combining measurement driven instruction with authentic assessment: the case of national assessment in England and Wales, *Educational Evaluation and Policy Analysis* 15(1): 81–90.

Whetton, C., Sainsbury, M., Hopkins, S., Ashby, J., Christopher, U., Clarke, J., Heath, M., Jones, G., Pulcher, J., Shagen, I. and Wilson, J. (1991) *An Evaluation of the 1991 National Curriculum Assessment, Report 1*. NFER/BGC Consortium. London: School Examinations and Assessment Council.

William, D. (1992) Some technical issues in assessment: a user's guide, *British Journal of Curriculum and Assessment* 2(2).

Wilson, M. (1992) Educational leverage from a political necessity. Implications of new perspectives on student assessment for chapter 1 evaluation, *Educational Evaluation and Policy Analysis* 14(2): 123–45.

Wolf, A. (1988) Assessing knowledge and understanding in National Vocational Qualifications. Report to the National Council for Vocational Qualifications, London.

Wolf, A. (1992) Delivery of national standards for training and development. Unpublished final report to the Department of Employment.

Wolf, A. (1993) *Assessment Issues and Problems in a Criterion-Referenced System*, Occasional Paper 2. London: Further Education Unit.

Wolf, A. and Silver, R. (1986) *Work-Based Learning: Trainee Assessment by Supervisors*, R & D Series No. 33. Sheffield: MSC.

Wood, R. (1986) The agenda for educational measurement. In D. L. Nuttall (ed.) *Assessing Educational Achievement*. Lewes: Falmer Press.

Wood, R. and Power, C. (1984) Have national assessments made us any wiser about standards?, *Comparative Education* 20(3): 307–21.

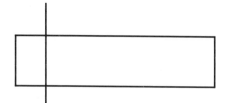

INDEX

ASSESSING ACHIEVEMENT IN THE ARTS

Malcolm Ross, Hilary Radnor, Sally Mitchell and Cathy Bierton

Largely absent from current assessment practice in the arts is any serious encouragement of the student's own act of self-appraisal: it is unusual for arts teachers to make time to sit down with individual students to talk about their creative work and help them weigh up their achievement. This is precisely the proposal made here. Following an intensive programme of collaborative research in ten secondary schools the authors set out the case for a fresh approach to assessment in the arts, an approach which gives the student a voice and at the same time allows the teacher access to the student's subjective world – that world in which particular aesthetic projects arise and unique aesthetic judgements are made. The vehicle of assessment becomes student-teacher talk: the reflective conversation. The research raises serious questions about the focus, emphasis and direction of the arts in education within the framework set out by the National Curriculum in the UK.

Contents
Contextualising the project – The project's history – Theoretical – Case studies – Conclusion – Notes – References and bibliography – Index.

192pp   0 335 19061 8 (Paperback)   0 335 19062 6 (hardback)

A FAIR TEST?
ASSESSMENT, ACHIEVEMENT AND EQUITY

Caroline Gipps and Patricia Murphy

How far is assessment fair? In this evaluation of research from a wide range of countries the authors examine the evidence for differences in performance among gender and ethnic groups on various forms of assessment. They explore the reasons put forward for these observed differences and clarify the issues involved. The authors' concern is that assessment practice and interpretation of results are *just* for all groups.

This is a complex field in which access to schooling, the curriculum offered, pupil motivation and esteem, teacher stereotype and expectation all interact with the mode of assessment. This analytical and comprehensive overview is essential reading in a field crucial to educators.

Contents
Introduction – Defining equity – Sex differences in intellectual abilities – Intelligence and intelligence testing – International surveys of achievement – National assessment programmes 1: the Assessment of Performance Unit in the UK – National assessment programmes 2: the National Assessment of Educational Progress in the USA – National Curriculum assessment – Examination performance – Conclusions: beyond the concept of a fair test – References – Index.

320pp   0 335 15673 8 (paperback)   0 335 15674 6 (hardback)

ASSESSING AND RECORDING ACHIEVEMENT
IMPLEMENTING A NEW APPROACH IN SCHOOL

Christopher J. Pole

Records of Achievement are meant to provide school students, parents and future employers with a document recognizing personal development and practical achievement; they are also seen as a challenge for teachers and pupils. Christopher Pole gives us an account of how Records of Achievement actually work through a case study of a particular school, and pays particular attention to the whole school nature of the endeavour and to pupil responses. He shows that there seems to be an almost irresistible pressure to bureaucratize the process of recording achievement in order for it to be integrated into the usual routines of schooling. This is then a cautionary tale for those who believe that schools are easily changed or controlled by changes in assessment. It makes fascinating reading for all those in schools and teacher training who are engaged in introducing new methods of assessment.

Contents

176pp   0 335 09960 2 (paperback)   0 335 09961 0 (hardback)